Future Global Shocks

IMPROVING RISK GOVERNANCE

OECD

This work is published on the responsibility of the Secretary-General of the OECD. The opinions expressed and arguments employed herein do not necessarily reflect the official views of the Organisation or of the governments of its member countries.

Please cite this publication as:

OECD (2011), *Future Global Shocks: Improving Risk Governance*, OECD Reviews of Risk Management Policies, OECD Publishing.
http://dx.doi.org/10.1787/9789264114586-en

ISBN 978-92-64-09520-5 (print)
ISBN 978-92-64-11458-6 (PDF)

Series: OECD Reviews of Risk Management Policies
ISSN 1993-4092 (print)
ISSN 1993-4106 (online)

Foreword

The International Futures Programme's project on "Future Global Shocks" originated in 2009 with a series of consultations among partners focusing on follow-up work to the decade-long research into risk management.

The awareness of risk management in government and the private sector has risen dramatically in recent years. Large-scale disasters have been recognised as challenges to public policy, usually at the national or regional level. The concept of "global shocks" takes account of a different pattern of risk: cascading risks that become active threats as they spread across global systems, whether these arise in health, climate, social or financial systems. Little work has been done on risks present in large-scale system interdependencies and the propagation of risks across global systems. Among the more important findings of this work for public policy is recognition that surveillance has now emerged as a key component in risk assessment and management. New knowledge management tools, modelling and data arrays provide unprecedented opportunities for anticipating some important global threats, and are increasingly sought by public policy managers worldwide. Secondly, there is a heightened role for security agencies in collaboration with regulatory agencies to use, adapt and implement risk-assessment tools in designing more resilient systems at the national and international levels. This report contributes directly to highlighting these new trends.

This report on future global shocks begins the next phase of OECD reviews of risk-management policies. In the wake of the 2008 financial crisis global leaders are acutely aware that another systemic shock could severely challenge economic recovery, social cohesion and even political stability. Visible indicators of vulnerability persist in the forms of economic imbalances, volatile commodity prices and currencies, colossal public debts and severe budget deficits. Quarterly indicators on economic recovery are closely scrutinised for signs of more chronic, structural weaknesses that place stress upon the social fabric, our final cushion of stability. Less visible than these metrics are the drivers of vulnerability that tightly weave interconnections between commercial supply chains, technological systems and investment vehicles underlying the global economy. Unanticipated events such as natural disasters, failures in key technical systems or malicious attacks could disrupt these complex systems and produce shocks that propagate around the world. There is a palpable sense of urgency to identify and assess risks arising from vulnerabilities in these crucial systems, and to develop policies that will bolster efforts for prevention, early warning and response to ensure sustained economic prosperity. This urgency explains the demand for OECD to deliver strategic advice on preparing for and responding to potential global shocks mired in uncertainties. While the list of potential global risks is quite long, this report focuses on a pressing shortlist, *i.e.* the relatively few that begin suddenly and result in severe, wide-scale disruptions or impacts.

The report draws primarily from analysis contained in five case studies on different types of events that could lead to global shocks, and a background paper that provides an overview of concepts, ideas, and examples of extreme events. All six background papers are available separately on the OECD website: *www.oecd.org/futures*. The report's contents are also based on input derived from consultations with the project's Steering Group and the results of independent research conducted by the OECD Secretariat. The Steering Group selected the case studies' topics on financial crises, pandemics and cyber risks for their potential to impact global systems and relevance in connection with recent events. The case studies on social unrest and geomagnetic storms were also commissioned to ensure that the report's conclusions were applicable to a broader range of events that might produce global shocks.

This report is part of the pioneering work of the International Futures Programme on risk. The OECD first began to analyse the policy implications of emerging and systemic risks in 1999 as part of its mission to build-up the organisation's foresight capacity. Since then, OECD countries have suffered major international terrorist attacks in 2001, 2003 and 2005, unprecedented destruction during hurricane Katrina in 2005, the worldwide financial meltdown in 2008 that reshaped and expanded the number of key constituents of global economic governance, the first declared pandemic in over 40 years in 2009, and most recently the Tohuku earthquakes, tsunami and ensuing nuclear reactor accidents at the Fukushima power plant. Never before have global risks seemed so complex, the stakes so high, and the need for international co-operation to deal with them so apparent. Throughout, the International Futures Programme has carried the torch in analysis of global risks along with its committed network of partners from government, industry, academia and civil society. In addition to its seminal report, "Emerging Risks in the 21st century: An Agenda for Action", and "Large-scale Disasters: Lessons Learned", it has published thematic reports and country case studies on the underlying economic, technological, environmental and social trends driving the emergence of global risks. The analysis and main conclusions from these publications hold true today, which underlines the need for policy makers to pay added attention to risks that are ever more present and ominous.

The Project team was composed of Michael Oborne, Barrie Stevens, Pierre Alain Schieb, David Sawaya, who contributed to chapters 2 and 3, and Jack Radisch, who was the principal author of the report. Pierre Alain Schieb, and Daniel Hoffman, then chief economist of Zurich Financial Services, developed some key concepts for the project; these were then discussed within the International Futures Programme and with other OECD partners with a view to launching a new project. The original Steering Group for the project included public and private sector participants as well as research professionals. Matthew Conroy developed the interesting "Tool Kit" for the project. Tom Van Nuffelen, Nadège Braure and Alexandra Hallas-Button provided valuable research assistance. Jennifer Stein and Gill O'Meara performed much appreciated copyediting and publication support, Peter Vogelpoel did the typesetting, and Anita Gibson and Rossella Iannizzotto provided logistics support. The Steering Group of the project met under my chairmanship over the 18-month period of the project.

Michael W. Oborne

Paris, June 2011

Table of contents

Figures

Tables

Boxes

Abbreviations

ABM	Agent-based models
CDC	Centers for Disease Control and Prevention
CI	Critical infrastructure
CERT	Computer Emergency Response Teams
CME	Coronal mass ejection
DDoS	Distributed Denial of Service
EFSF	European Financial Stability Facility
ENISA	European Network Security Agency
FSAP	Financial Sector Assessment Program
FSB	Financial Stability Board
GICs	Geomagnetically induced currents
GIS	Geographic information systems
GISN	Global Influenza Surveillance Network
GOARN	Global Outbreak Alert and Response Network
GPS	Global Positioning System
ICT	Information and communication technology
IEA	International Energy Agency
IHR	International Health Regulations
IMF	International Monetary Fund
IMPACT	International Multilateral Partnership Against Cyber Threats
IRGC	International Risk Governance Council
ISES	International Space Environment Service
ITU	International Telecommunications Union
NAS	National Academy of Sciences
OAS	Organization of American States
OSPR	California Office of Spill Prevention & Response
RWC	Regional Space Weather Warning Centres
SCADA	Supervisory control and data acquisition

SSN	Safe Sea Net
SWPC	Space Weather Prediction Center
TARP	Troubled Asset Relief Program
WHO	World Health Organization
WMO	World Meteorological Organization

Chapter 1

Definition and drivers of future global shocks

Extremely disruptive events, such as earthquakes, volcanoes, financial crises and political revolutions destabilise critical systems of supply, producing economic spillovers that reach far beyond their geographical point of origin. While such extreme events have been relatively rare in the past, they seem poised to occur with greater frequency in the future. Global interconnections accompanying economic integration enable some risks to propagate rapidly around the world. What do governments and multinational businesses need to do to prepare for the ripple effects of such events and to limit their negative consequences? The OECD International Futures Programme has completed an 18-month study on future global shocks, which took stock of the challenges in assessing, preventing and responding to several potential global risks. The working definition of "Global Shock" and several of the most important enabling drivers are presented here.

Introduction

Recent global shocks, such as the 2008 financial crisis, have driven policy makers and industry strategists to re-examine how to prepare for and respond to such systemic shock events in the future, whether they arise in financial, natural, technological, social or even political systems. This report provides strategic guidance to address systemic shocks, and outlines several common challenges confronting efforts to manage them. Global shocks can arise from an event that impacts the entire world more or less at once, such as the collision of the earth with a massive asteroid, or they may result from more subtle events that begin locally and spread to distant points around the world. What allows for the latter type of event to spread are the interconnections and interdependencies embedded in the networks that characterise the modern global economy. There are a wide range of such networks through which risks may spread globally, *e.g.* financial markets, the Internet or simply aeroplanes carrying passengers who are infected with a dangerous virus.

While these networks enable local impacts to propagate across multiple territories, production systems, industries and asset classes, societies generally accept them as necessary for the improvements they bring to living standards. As dependence on these networks increases gradually, so too do vulnerabilities, which may be difficult to understand or foresee sufficiently in advance to prevent or counteract. Even when an organisation does anticipate shock events that exploit these vulnerabilities, it may lack the knowledge, tools or means to take effective action or to warn the public. Moreover, there is often little incentive for individuals to take a systemic view that examines interconnections and interdependencies between different parts or agents of a complex system. Most observers tend to focus on protecting the system component for which it is responsible or has a direct interest. As a consequence the likelihood and secondary effects of disruptive events often remain unknown, unmapped and generally unprepared for.

The term "extreme events" has become popular to describe the most infrequent forms of disasters marked by uncertainty. Experts often apply statistical terms to describe such relative rarity with more precision, for example by labelling particular events as lying along the fat tail of a distribution curve or as a 1 in 10 000-year disaster. Due to the uncertainties surrounding probability of occurrence and extent of impact, so-called extreme events present substantial challenges for risk managers (Casti, 2010). The aim of this report is to advance understanding of how to improve global capacity to confront sudden and highly disruptive threats, given the unknowns and uncertainties that pervade their occurrence, causal linkages and the resistance thresholds of systems they impact upon. The report indicates gaps in various governance capacities and suggests courses of corrective action, ranging from the diversification and/or redundancy of complex systems where economically feasible, to the cultivation of societal resilience when they are not.

What are future global shocks?

The working definition of future global shocks in this report is: a rapid onset event with severely disruptive consequences covering at least two continents. While many events may result in national level disasters that require international assistance, most do not produce secondary or knock-on effects across multiple continents, and therefore do not rise to the level of a future global shock. Of course there are often relevant lessons to be drawn from these experiences. Some national level disasters are important precursors to global shocks and should not be ignored, but rather incite analysis to ascertain economic, technological and social interconnections that hold potential as vectors for broader scale disruption. Such vectors are most likely to result in propagation when a rapid sequence of events converges with poorly governed vulnerabilities.

The models for aggregate supply and demand can help visualise rudimentary economic impacts of negative shocks. Figure 1.1 illustrates a negative supply-side shock, an example of which followed the July 2010 wildfires in Russia that eventually destroyed a fifth of its wheat crops (Russia is the world's third largest wheat exporter). The wildfires occurred in conjunction with a record drought that had already threatened the country's crop harvests. Subsequently, Russia decided to halt wheat exports, which resulted in sharp fluctuations in grain prices in agriculture commodities markets (a shift from AS1 to AS2; with equilibrium changing from A to B). Near the same time there had been massive floods in Australia, Canada and the United States that reduced global supplies. Significant structural changes to global demand were also underway with booming economic growth in China and India, causing a shift from AD1 to AD2, and equilibrium to shift from B to C). The temporary influence of the Russian export ban was further exacerbated by hoarding in some countries for fear that another food crisis may be looming (a shift from AS2 to AS3; and equilibrium shifted from point C to D). In North Africa fermenting public sentiment rooted in repressive and unaccountable leaders, recent Internet penetration, a demographic "youth bulge" and relatively high unemployment pushed social stability towards a tipping point. The effects of rapid and multiple price hikes combined with these chronic conditions triggered social unrest, which in turn spurred contagion effects in Egypt, Libya and throughout several countries in the Middle East and North Africa region (Apps, 2011).

The aggregate model in Figure 1.1 describes, but does not explain, the underlying dynamics driving the shifts indicated. The process of aggregation and functional dependency between various aggregates needs to be interpreted statistically and validated. Nor does this static model allow policy makers and risk managers to anticipate and prepare for such shocks before they happen. To brace themselves for the effects of such extreme events, risk managers can sometimes fortify or diversify their assets that are exposed due to interconnections with or dependency on the disrupted supply. Reaction time is of the essence to preventing or minimising future global shocks and distinguishes them from the risks

Figure 1.1. **Supply-side shocks**

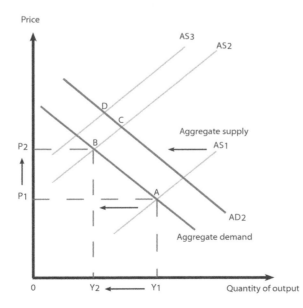

national governments, businesses and society at large are accustomed to. For this reason, risk managers need to develop maps that depict functional interconnections and models that produce a probability of the transmission of risks through complex and interdependent systems (Jovanovic *et al.*, 2011). Such tools are the foundation for early warning systems that could be used to activate policy interventions to contain risks before they spread to different sectors and multiply losses.

The future is now

Shocks in the future may arise from previously unknown hazards for which there are no data and no model for likelihood and impacts; the so-called unknown-unknown events (Casti, 2010). Global shocks caused by an entirely novel hazard, *e.g.* long return period comets, are less emphasised in this report than known hazards that interact with previously unknown or unprepared-for vulnerabilities. How these latter events propagate through the intense bundling of interdependencies in today's world, and what to do about them, is the focus of this report. Interdependencies are in great part a result of the global economy's pursuit of ever-increasing scale, which achieve efficiencies and perhaps increase profits, but also create ominous externalities for society. A principal benefit of international co-operation to stem global shocks would be to agree on incentives for actors to internalise such costs or otherwise take into account the external effects of their actions that increase society's vulnerability.

Managing unknown-unknowns might seem like guesswork, but there are several strategic concepts available to aid risk managers. Generally, this involves a combination of two techniques:

1. Designing or reinforcing complex systems to be more robust, redundant and/or diverse as appropriate; and

2. Building societal resilience to unknown events by drawing from experience with extreme events that share some similarity in nature or scale.

To coherently manage such widespread vulnerabilities there is a need to integrate decision-making processes, lest some policies continue to support activities that potentially create enormous external costs. In addition, to identify and prepare for events that might exploit such vulnerabilities requires knowing what externalities are being produced beyond national borders, and eventually co-ordinating policies at the international level to reduce them. In the same way that multilateral alliances can create the conditions for increased trade with economic benefits as spill over effects, so too can international co-operation attempt to fine-tune policies to reduce the risk of future global shocks.

Global shocks know no boundaries

As mentioned above, future global shocks exhibit the potential for wide-ranging, destructive consequences that transcend national boundaries. In addition to macroeconomic shocks that traverse globally integrated markets, sudden food shortages, natural disasters and outbreaks of infectious disease may occur in faraway places, yet quickly produce secondary effects that disrupt various industrial and social systems around the world. A key challenge to managing future global shocks, therefore, is to identify and better understand how they propagate and produce devastating knock-on effects. This is a precursor to higher orders of international co-operation such as the establishment of prevention frameworks or control points.

Finally, future global shocks face unique challenges due to their speed of onset. Not unlike a pure electrical shock, a global shock entails a rapid-onset event with initial impacts or consequences for a particular entity or system that spread quickly and often outpace policy interventions to control them. By way of opposition, risks related to climate change and longevity are typically slow-onset and do not represent a shock scenario (unless of course a tipping point is reached that makes impacts unfold very quickly). This distinction is important as slow-onset risks, although certainly capable of similar degrees of damage or consequence, provide more time for society to adjust, react, and mitigate risk before, during and after onset. Shocks occur suddenly, with little or no warning, providing a uniquely strenuous test for emergency management and society's resilience.

Are future global shocks only negative?

Discussions of large-scale threats to global stability almost always consider a shock to be a serious negative blow to a vital system or economic sector. Two important qualifications to the popular view should be noted. First, the consequences of a shock are often a matter of perspective; an event with negative outcomes for one party can create opportunities for a different party. Second, some events taken at face value are clearly positive shocks. The development of new technologies, for example, may increase the productivity of a representative bundle of inputs and have been shown to account for the bulk of aggregate economic growth. In Figure 1.2 the technology shock increases output, given the same level of labour input. The marginal product of labour (MPL) line is higher after the positive technology shock, which can be seen in its steeper slope. Technology shocks are events in a macroeconomic model that change the production function.

The invention of a cheap, clean and renewable energy supply could radically alter the course of international trade balances, while medical breakthroughs such as personalised medicine promise to increase the efficacy and safety of medications and eventually the

Figure 1.2. **Technology shocks**

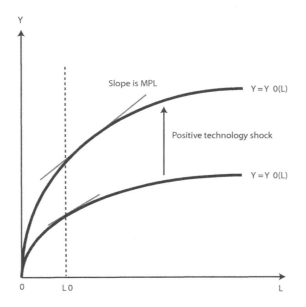

Note: An example of the function, where Y = output, L = labour, MPL = Marginal product of labour.

average human life span. In addition to their benefits, both examples would produce shocks to current models of economic activity and public finances. Recognition of potential future shocks invites creativity, collaboration, the use of technological advances to meet global challenges, and furtherance of filling current gaps in governance architectures.

Drivers of future global shocks

Strategies that manage global shocks need to distinguish between the immediate risks that trigger a shock and the more chronic, underlying drivers. The former require prompt tactical interventions at key propagation points, whereas the latter involve longer-term strategies to identify and diffuse situations headed towards tipping points. A risk is an uncertain consequence of an event or an activity with regard to something humans value (Kates *et al.*, 1985). A driver is an aspect of society, the economy or environment that effects a change on another aspect of these systems (IRGC, 2010). In the infectious diseases field, for example, a pathogen might or might not harm infected plants, animals and/or people, all of which hold value for humans. There are many drivers of infectious diseases, such as urbanisation, land use, loss of biodiversity and climate change that alter the conditions under which pathogens could mutate and become more or less infective, transmissible and virulent. Integrated approaches to dealing with future global shocks should address not only a specific risk, but also understand the context of any underlying drivers. There are five key macro drivers in particular that augment vulnerability and amplify consequences, making future global shocks more likely:

Heightened mobility

Increased mobility is most obvious in the growth of information and capital flows, migration, international tourism and business travel. The trend in trading goods continues to move towards greater quantities than ever. Despite a major economic contraction in 2009, over USD12 trillion worth of goods and USD 3 trillion of services were exported

Figure 1.3. **Broadband penetration rates in OECD countries, 2010**

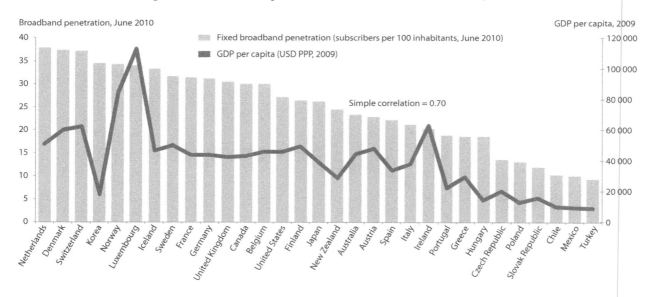

Source: OECD (2010), Broadband penetration and GDP, June, available at *www.oecd.org/sti/ict/broadband.*

worldwide, and exports have been growing faster than production since the 1980s (WTO, 2010). This ratio has increased steadily since 1985, and jumped by nearly one-third between 2000 and 2008. Meanwhile, intense data transfer via the Internet has revolutionised the global economy with OECD countries seeing a 550% rise in Internet users from 1997-2007 (see Figure 1.3). Supporting development of these trends for the past 20 years have been significant gains in transport efficiency, political stability and market openness.

The unprecedented flow of data, people and commercial transactions has simultaneously increased economic opportunities and the potential for risks to propagate. Resembling an invasive species, some threats, particularly infectious diseases, follow the people, animals and information systems that have been infected. With more carriers on the move and connected to an increasing number of potential hosts, risks are being introduced to markets, industrial production systems, information networks and social communities where countermeasures may be scarce and resilience underdeveloped.

Figure 1.4. **Bot-infected computers per 100 broadband subscribers, December 2006**

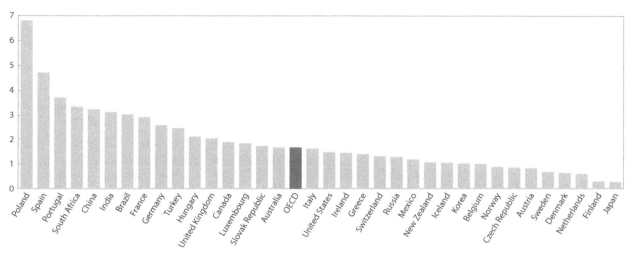

Note: The columns represent the number of infected computers per 100 broadband subscribers in OECD countries.

Source: OECD (2007), *OECD Science, Technology and Industry: Scoreboard 2007*, OECD Publishing, Paris.

Interdependency of production and delivery systems and their infrastructure

The operations of several infrastructure systems that support modern economies and provide basic services to their societies have become increasingly interconnected, especially via information and communications technology (ICT). Communications systems are the backbone for much of the critical infrastructure, thus any disruption to its architecture is potentially a threat to a broad range of critical services. As Figure 1.5 shows there is a great deal of interdependency between communications systems and critical infrastructure sectors. Every node in the communications architecture – whether it is a switching centre, radio relay site, cell site, or remote site – relies on electrical power for its operation. In most cases, the power to run the communications infrastructure is provided on a continual basis by the commercial power industry. The energy sector is comprised of the oil, gas, and electric power production, refining, storage and distribution facilities. As such, there is a direct and critical link between the electrical power networks and the communications networks that are dependent on them. On the other hand, the electrical power industry is dependent upon the communications providers for inter-facility communications, management and control of operations, and management of facilities.

Figure 1.5. **Critical infrastructure interdependencies**

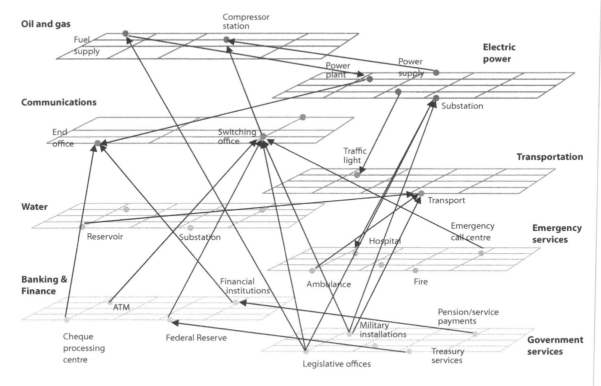

Source: NARUC (The National Association of Regulatory Utility Commissioners) (2005), *Utility and Network Interdependencies: What State Regulators Need to Know, Technical Assistance Brief on Critical Infrastructure Protection*, Washington, DC, available at *www.naruc.org/Publications/CIP_Interdependencies_2.pdf.*

Centralisation and concentration of systems

Concentration, if not centralisation, has become an important facet of efficiency for transportation hubs and financial payments. As a network structure, a hub allows greater flexibility within the transport system and transaction speed within the financial payment system. If a major hub is disrupted, however, delays may ripple through interconnected supply chains. This not only upsets the functioning of the tightly knit transportation and financial payment sectors, it induces volatility that may lead to losses in productivity, foreign investment and access to exports, whether they be food, water, electricity, productive capital or some other scarce resource. Part of the challenge in preparing for and managing the risk of future global shocks is to diversify these hubs or to build-in greater system robustness and redundancy.

For example, there are four major air freight carriers that account for the bulk of global air cargo. Each has a hub-and-spoke organisation of their network with hubs clustered around the world's three major zones of economic activity; North America, Europe and Pacific Asia. The choice of the main consolidation hub is based upon an airport that is well located, has good infrastructure, but that does not service a very large local passenger market to ensure it is the airport's main customer and receives privileged access to the runways. There is a high level of concentration of hubs in the Eastern part of the United States, which roughly corresponds to its demographic concentration. Disruptions to this hub result in bottlenecks and delivery delays to the rest of the continent.

Figure 1.6. **Global hubs for air freight transport**

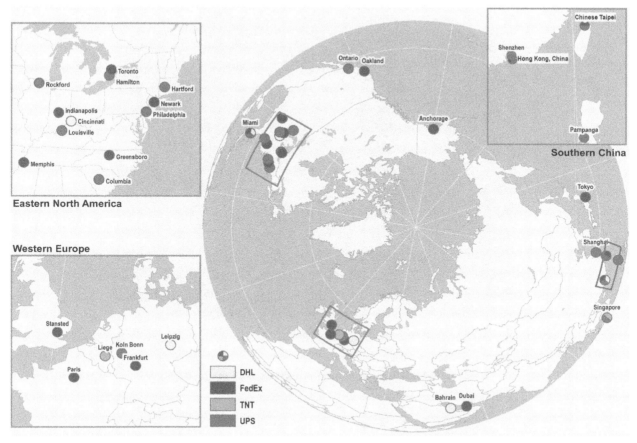

Source: Rodrigue, J.P., Comtois, C. and Slack, B. (2009), The Geography of Transport Systems, Second Edition, Routledge, New York, p. 30 (image available at http://*people.hofstra.edu/geotrans/eng/ch5en/appl5en/img/Map_Air_Freight_Integrators.pdf*; copyright © 2009 J.P. Rodrigue).

When a volcanic eruption in Iceland produced an ash cloud over the air space of Europe's major air hubs in 2010, many companies were unable to deliver products or key components to markets and production systems throughout Europe (see Figure 1.7). The event was an opportunity to consider many questions relevant to policy makers and businesses alike, for example: What level of diversification would be required to maintain current supply capacity if the eruption had continued and air space had been closed for a month, a year or even longer? What technologies could be implemented to better inform risk analysis, and avoid blanket closures of air space in the future? In the short term, the major effects of closing air space were mostly limited to losses for airlines, stranded passengers, delayed orders for manufacturing and lost orders for sellers trying to export perishable goods to European markets. In a longer lasting scenario, global trade and especially Europe might suffer massive losses.

Urbanisation and concentration of populations and assets

The increasing urbanisation of the world population has resulted in an increasing number of megacities with high concentrations of both people and assets in relatively small, compact areas. With such dense convergence of populations and collective wealth into

Figure 1.7. **The 2010 volcanic ash cloud over European airspace**

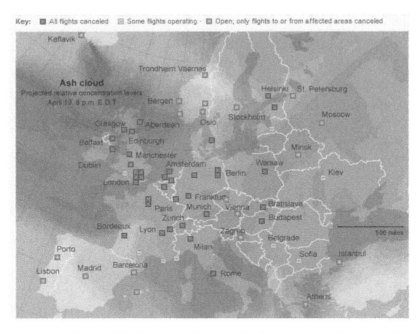

Source: Brandt, J., National Environmental Research Institute at Aarhus University, Denmark.

Figure 1.8. **Concentration of populations in megacities**

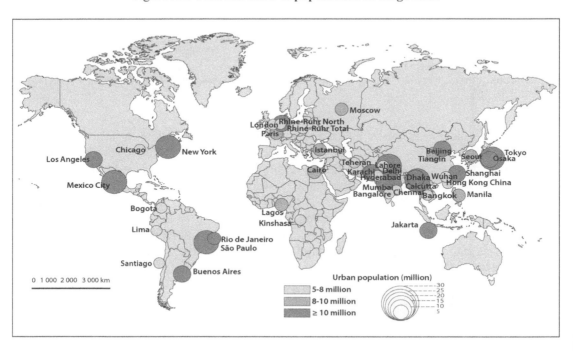

Source: UN (2002), Draft and copyright: Frauke Krass, Cartography: R. Spohner, MegaCity Taskforce of the International Geographical Union, Department of Geography, University of Cologne. Map available at: *www.megacities.uni-koeln.de/documentation/*.

geographic centres, the risk of a catastrophic event producing irreparable damage and loss is significantly increased. Similar to the logic of the increased interconnectivity of infrastructure, high concentrations of population and resources in urban centres both present potential sites of greater calamity due to natural hazards and attractive targets to nefarious attacks. Although more can be done to increase society's resilience and communicate more effectively with these populations about the risks they face, expected population growth will only exacerbate the trend toward urbanisation in the future.

Herd behaviour and "groupthink" in corporations and professions and among regulators

A common principle of risk management is to be aware of cognitive biases and not to expect the future to be like the past. In some large organisations, whether firms or bureaucracies, a frequent dynamic is for executives to leave operational responsibility to middle managers without sufficient supervision to know the details of the risks possibly confronting the organisation's mission. The incentive for middle managers to create a friendly working environment may override critical appraisal of their subordinate's performance. In such environments there is often a lack of critical thinking about operating procedures and assumptions underlying legacy models that might have been appropriate in the past, but have long outlived their productive capacity. Risks to the organisation's mission a re not ignored so much as they are simply not perceived. A similar dynamic can infiltrate professions, where members continue to think according to the analytical methods and decision rules in which they have received common training.

The broad-sweeping trends described above introduce just a few of the most important critical issues that contribute to a greater likelihood of future global shocks. There are many other trends that increase vulnerability, such as growing income disparities that render society's impoverished less resilient to shock events. The high degree of uncertainty about the likelihood of future global shocks and the pervasive feeling of insecurity this creates among the general public have powerful implications for risk governance both by countries and businesses.

First, uncertainty complicates the tasks of building adequate capacities for prediction, prevention/mitigation, and response/continuity planning, which can lead to untimely reactions, misguided preparations, and disproportionate reactions. Second, uncertainty can undermine the sense of urgency so often needed for the support of decision-makers to invest in these capacities. Persistent deficiencies in these capacities can weaken society's trust in the public sector's ability, and private sector's willingness, to manage risks and respond to large-scale disruptions. This fact underlines the great importance of analysing the specific challenges global shocks raise for improving risk communication. Third, the general public in OECD countries holds policy makers, the public sector in general and critical services to an increasingly high standard in its risk-management efforts. It is not sufficient for risk managers to limit losses from disruptions; the public also expects efficiency from state services and utilities, and wants to know that the interventions are cost-effective. As a result, greater research and development efforts are required to provide the theoretical and data-driven support for risk management strategies within government as a means to bolster more holistic approaches to managing systemic risks.

The 21st century is likely to see more global shocks, some familiar, others new, due to a rapidly changing environment where the one reliable constant is its increasing conduciveness to shocks. The following chapters consider what challenges and implications the current risk landscape, framed by the drivers described above, implies for efforts to improve the governance of future global shocks. They draw common lessons from the project case studies on the topics of risk assessment (Chapter 2); tools to prepare for future global shocks –including mapping and modelling (Chapter 3); and emergency management (Chapter 4). A final section considers elements of a strategic approach to building resilience for global shocks (Chapter 5).

Bibliography

Apps, P. (2011), *Analysis: After the crisis, a worldwide rise in unrest,* Thomson Reuters, London.

Briguglio, L. *et al.* (2005), "Conceptualizing and Measuring Economic Resilience", Pacific Islands Regional Integration and Governance, ANU Press, Canberra, pp. 26-49.

Casti, J. (2011), *Future Global Shocks: Four Faces of Tomorrow*, OECD, Paris.

Diekmann, N. *et al.* (2008), *CRO briefing: Emerging Risks Initiative – Position Paper: The Digital Economy's Achilles' heel*, Critical Information Infrastructure, Amstelveen.

Douple, E.B. *et al.* (2011), "Long-term Radiation-Related Health Effects in a Unique Human Population: Lessons Learned from the Atomic Bomb Survivors of Hiroshima and Nagasaki", *Disaster Medicine and Public Health Preparedness*, Vol. 5, Supplement 1, American Medical Association, pp. 122-133.

Dunn, M. (2007), "Critical Infrastructures: Vulnerabilities, Threats, Responses", *CSS Analyses in Security Policy*, Vol. 2, No. 16, Zurich.

Ellwood, P. *et al.* (2011), *Foresight of New and Emerging Risks on Occupational Safety and Health Associated with New Technologies in Green Jobs by 2020*, European Agency for Safety and Health at Work, Luxembourg.

Falconer, A., J. Hyde and J. Perks (2009) *Study on Risk Governance of European Critical Infrastructures in the ICT and Energy Sector*, AEA, European Commission, Oxfordshire.

Gaïa, D. and P. Nouvel (2006), *Sécurité et compagnies aériennes*, Éditions du Puits Fleuri.

Gaspard, F. and A. Hubrecht (2010), *Tackling Critical Energy Infrastructure Network Interdependencies*, European Centre for Critical Infrastructure Protection.

Graham, J.D. *et al.* (2010), *The Emergence of Risks: Contributing Factors, International Risk Governance Council*, Geneva.

Heller, M. (2001), "Interdependencies in Civil Infrastructure Systems", *The Bridge*, Vol. 31, No. 4, National Academy of Engineering, Washington, DC.

Institut Pierre Simon Laplace (Université de Versailles Saint-Quentin) (2010), LATMOS, "Suivi des émissions de cendres du volcan islandais Eyjafjöll", 20 April.

IRGC (International Risk Governance Council) (2010), *The Emergence of Risks Contributing Factors*, IRGC, Geneva.

Jovanovic, A., O. Renn and R. Schröter (2011), *Social Unrest*, OECD Project on Future Global Shocks, OECD, Paris.

Kambhu J., N. Krishnan and S. Weidman (2007), *New Directions for Understanding Systemic Risk: A Report on a Conference Cosponsored by the Federal Reserve Bank of New York and the National Academy of Sciences*, The National Academies Press, Washington, DC.

Kates, R.W., C. Hohenemser and J. Kasperson (1985), *Perilous Progress: Managing the Hazards of Technology*, Westview Press, Boulder.

Ministry of the Interior and Kingdom Relations (2009), "Mega-crises in the 21st century", *National Safety & Security and Crisis Management Magazine*, Special issue October 2009, The Hague.

Net Security (2008), "Critical infrastructure is not prepared for cyber attacks", *www.net-security.org/secworld.php?id=6727*.

NSTAC (National Security Telecommunications Advisory Committee) (2003), *Vulnerabilities Task Force Report: Concentration of assets: Telecom Hotels*, NSTAC, Washington, DC.

Rodrigue, J-P *et al.* (2009) *The Geography of Transport Systems*, Hofstra University, Department of Global Studies & Geography, accessed 5 November 2010, *http://people. hofstra.edu/geotrans*.

Serfling, R.E. (1963), "Methods for Current Statistical Analysis of Excess Pneumonia-influenza Deaths", *Public Health Reports*, Vol. 78, No. 6, pp. 194-506.

The Economist (2011), "Risk Radar 2011: How firms are navigating risk", *Economist Intelligence Unit Report*, London.

WEF (World Economic Forum) (2011) (Global Risks 2011), Sixth edition: "An Initiative of the Risk Response Network", WEF, Geneva.

WTO (World Trade Organization) (2010), PRESS/598, International trade statistics, 26 March.

Chapter 2

Risk assessments for future global shocks

To assess the probability and consequence of future global shocks a better under-standing is needed about where contagion effects and amplification are likely to occur. First, risk managers must identify the hubs of critical systems and resources, which if disrupted could trigger a series of adverse knock-on effects. They also need to investigate how dependency on a single or few critical resources or systems may create unexpected vulnerabilities to endogenous or exogenous shocks. In addition, risk managers should adopt a broader view of risk, beyond visible direct threats, and expand their situation awareness to include trends and events that take place in far away locations and identify components in critical systems that may amplify risks. This chapter focuses on the potential for global shocks resulting from the threats covered in the project's case studies on pandemics, financial crises, cyber risks and geomagnetic storms. It draws general conclusions regarding the need to increase access to data and information resources in order to establish or reinforce systemic risk assessments.

Introduction

Global shocks are similar to any form of risk in that they arise from a convergence between hazards and vulnerabilities to hazards. The principle differences between global shocks and local or even national level shocks are the interconnected pathways through which risks can accumulate, propagate and culminate in a much greater scale of effects, and the uncertainties surrounding their likelihood of occurrence. Yet, to make informed decisions on any type of risk, an organisation requires some consideration of the frequency of an unwanted event (such as for a natural hazard) or indicators that an event may occur (such as for a terrorist attack). When it comes to global shocks, risk managers need to take a systemic perspective to risk assessment that looks at the causal relations of contagion and the total impacts of direct and indirect costs. By taking a broader view than the most apparent hazards and vulnerabilities risk managers may avoid their goals from being compromised indirectly, for example, by dependency on a source or system that is itself vulnerable to endogenous or exogenous (internal or external) shocks.

Network systems theory lends a number of relevant insights to the task of assessing risks of future global shocks. A complex system can collapse if a disruption occurs in a sufficient number of nodes around which the system is organised. Figure 2.1 depicts a simplified network diagram in which a failed hub (dark blue) has initiated contagion to failing nodes (light blue), which threaten to contaminate the rest of the nodes in the network (white). Risk assessment for global shocks should begin with assessment of nodes in identified critical systems and focus first on collection and analysis of data about the exposure of nodes upon which society is most dependent. Second, vulnerability analysis should be conducted upon the nodes most likely to extend contagion effects. In most cases this will be a network's hubs, which are nodes with the greatest proportion of total inter-linkages. If a major hub is disrupted, contaminated or compromised, a risk assessment should be performed to determine the potential for contagion to the nodes upon which it is connected. The case studies on pandemics, financial crises, cyber risks, geomagnetic storms and social unrest illustrate the propagation of threats in three systems essential to the security and prosperity of society: public health, finance and the critical infrastructure sectors of telecommunications and energy.

Figure 2.1. **Basic contagion diagram: nodes and hubs**

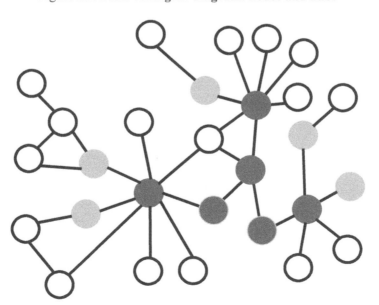

The risks described in this chapter have the potential to disrupt complex, interconnected systems and thereby cause massive international impacts. Whether they produce global shocks, however depends on the simultaneous presence of various conditions. Arguably, financial crises both occur more frequently and produce more severe monetary damage than the other types of risks described. There is concern therefore that the tools for risk analysis have not worked as well, and that policy makers seem less able to understand, analyse, model, predict and prevent these types of shock. A main difference between financial crises and the other forms of shock discussed below is that they result from non-malicious, human choices. For the other types of shock discussed the proximate cause is a natural event, accident or malicious act. This difference highlights the assumption found in many neo-classical economic models that humans act in rational self-interest, and underlines the need for a new generation of models that use data on how agents actually behave.

Despite this important difference, the risks described below share several commonalities, which underscore the practical difficulty decision-makers face to enhance governance capacity to deal with them. After all, systemic risk is not only an issue for financial systems; it also appears in technical and social systems as an undesired externality arising from the strategic interaction of agents (Lorenz, J., 2009). First, identifying the most vulnerable hubs in some of these systems is painstakingly difficult, and those that have been identified are not always easy to isolate for the purpose of preventive and/or protective action. Second, progress is needed in modelling the estimated return periods of hazards of sufficient force that can set off significant knock-on effects or even chain reactions. In other words, there is great uncertainty both about where and when they will occur. Third, the regular conduct of independent and validated stress tests in complex systems is rare. Fourth, it is difficult to accurately capture the total attributable economic impacts of disruptions to complex systems, which leads to consideration of risk amplifiers in the following section.

Table 2.1. **Features of potential global shocks**

Global shock	Hazard	Precursors	Uncertainties	Global vectors	Frequency
Pandemic	Human influenza	National epidemic threshold exceeded	Location and timing of onset, attack rate, morbidity and mortality	Travel in aeroplanes, wild aquatic birds	μ ~30 years
Critical Infrastructure Disruption	Zero day exploit of virus or worm code	Terrorist threats made in advance	Cross-border interdependencies	Internet, USB keys, DVD, CD, floppy disk	?
Financial Crisis	Massive bank illiquidity/ insolvencies, currency crisis, sovereign default	Asset bubbles, sudden rise in spread of bank rates	Amounts of bank debt exposures	Interconnections of bank debt holdings, common currencies and pegged currencies	?
Geomagnetic storm	Geomagnetically induced current	Coronal mass ejection	Ranges of latitude exposed to direct impacts	Critical infrastructure disruptions	Peaks during 11-year solar cycle
Social unrest	Political revolt or revolution	Riots, protest demonstrations	Duration, severity, credibility	Affiliation of political, religious or cultural identity	?

Pandemics

A pandemic is defined in reference to an epidemic, which is generally held to occur when new cases of a certain disease, in a given human population, and during a given period, substantially exceed what is expected based on recent experience. A few concentrated cases of a rare, contagious disease may be considered an epidemic, while many dispersed cases of a common disease (such as the common cold) would not. An epidemic may be restricted to one locale, or it may be global, in which case it is a pandemic. There is no generally accepted threshold between these two extremes, above which an epidemic should be called a pandemic. For influenza WHO provides a six-phase staggered system, culminating in the declaration of a pandemic described in Table 2.2.

Public health authorities contend with many uncertainties when determining whether a disease outbreak is an epidemic, such as its attack rate, morbidity and mortality. How these uncertainties are managed influences potentially onerous risk prevention and mitigation measures, *e.g.* social distancing measures and how to prioritise the distribution of vaccines. Reducing the uncertainties surrounding risk assessment and thereby improving the cost-effectiveness and equity of responses is a challenge. When novel viruses or bacteria causing food borne illness are identified such uncertainties may lead some decision-makers

Table 2.2. **WHO Six phases of pandemic declaration**

INTER-PANDEMIC PERIOD	
1	No viruses circulating among animals have been reported to cause infections in humans.
2	An animal virus circulating among domesticated or wild animals is known to have caused infection in humans, and is therefore considered a potential pandemic threat.
PANDEMIC ALERT PERIOD	
3	An animal or human-animal influenza reassortant virus has caused sporadic cases or small clusters of disease in people, but has not resulted in human-to-human transmission sufficient to sustain community-level outbreaks. Limited human-to-human transmission may occur under some circumstances, for example, when there is close contact between an infected person and an unprotected caregiver. However, limited transmission under such restricted circumstances does not indicate that the virus has gained the level of transmissibility among humans necessary to cause a pandemic.
4	Verified human-to-human transmission of an animal or human-animal virus able to cause "community-level outbreaks". The ability to cause sustained disease outbreaks in a community marks a significant upwards shift in the risk for a pandemic. Any country that suspects or has verified such an event should urgently consult with WHO so that the situation can be jointly assessed and a decision made by the affected country if implementation of a rapid pandemic containment operation is warranted. Phase 4 indicates a significant increase in risk of a pandemic but does not necessarily mean that a pandemic is a foregone conclusion.
5	Human-to-human spread of the virus into at least two countries in one WHO region. While most countries will not be affected at this stage, the declaration of Phase 5 is a strong signal that a pandemic is imminent and that the time to finalise the organisation, communication, and implementation of the planned mitigation measures is short.
PANDEMIC PERIOD	
6	Community level outbreaks in at least one other country in a different WHO region in addition to the criteria defined in Phase 5. Designation of this phase will indicate that a global pandemic is under way.
Post-Peak Period	Levels of pandemic influenza in most countries with adequate surveillance have dropped below peak levels. During this period additional waves of the pandemic may recur.
Post-Pandemic Period	Levels of influenza activity have returned to the levels seen for seasonal influenza in most countries with adequate surveillance.

Source: Adapted from WHO, "WHO Pandemic Phase Descriptions and Main Actions by Phase", available at: *www.who.int/csr/disease/influenza/pandemic_phase_descriptions_and_actions.pdf.*

to impulsive responses while others may wait too long to act. Ill informed decisions about the source or severity of an outbreak may lead to ineffective countermeasures that can have significant economic consequences that are difficult to remedy.

Though it is impossible to predict the exact timing or nature of any future pandemic, experts agree that the most likely virus to reach pandemic proportions will be a novel form of influenza A, for which there is little or no immunity in the human population, and that spreads easily from person-to-person. Strains of influenza are always circulating somewhere in the world; the virus has a seasonal occurrence in temperate climates, while it occurs year-round in the tropics. In the northern hemisphere, the season usually starts in November or December and subsides before May. In the Southern Hemisphere, it usually begins in May and subsides by October. Most professionals in public health, medicine and epidemiology consider the next flu pandemic to be inevitable, but they do not know precisely when or where it will begin. Over the past three centuries, a flu pandemic has been identified every 25 to 30 years on average. Three influenza pandemics occurred during the 20th Century: 1918-19, 1957-58, and 1968-69. Perhaps due to the emergence of H5N1 avian influenza, most experts had expected the next flu pandemic to begin in Southeast Asia, which made the 2008 H1N1 pandemic that emerged in Mexico an unexpected surprise.

The most severe influenza pandemic of the 20th century occurred in 1918-19 when an estimated 40 to 50 million deaths were caused worldwide. The WHO considers 2 to 7.4 million deaths globally as a conservative estimate of an H5N1 avian flu pandemic, with substantial effects on both the physical and financial health of countries. Forecasting the severity of an actual outbreak's impacts, however, is wrought with uncertainties. Early on in an outbreak, epidemiological models are used to forecast impacts by projecting attack and fatality rates drawn from laboratory confirmation of suspected cases. Data on confirmed cases becomes increasingly difficult to acquire while a pandemic continues, not only because it is expensive to administer diagnostics to so many people, but also because people are afraid to go to clinics for fear of becoming infected. In most influenza outbreaks the most severe impacts are concentrated at both ends of the age spectrum; the very young and the elderly, although younger populations, such as school children, may have the highest attack rates. Persons with certain underlying chronic illnesses are also at higher risk of serious complications from influenza compared to the general population. The age distribution of illnesses and fatalities is an important factor in quantifying the longer term economic impacts of infectious diseases.

Shortly before the H1N1 influenza pandemic, several studies were conducted to estimate the economic costs that would arise from fatalities, hospitalisation and medical treatments. Influenza pandemics, however, result not only in such direct costs, but also in indirect costs such as absenteeism and associated productivity losses. During a pandemic, shocks to supply are expected in transport, trade, payment systems, and major utilities (IMF, 2006). Tourist destinations that suffer high infection rates or are made inaccessible due to travel restrictions are likely to suffer negative demand shocks. If two-way trade flows are not restricted, imports in some countries may rise on account of a greater need for medical goods and services, although this may be offset by sharply lower domestic demand and production. A separate study positing a pandemic that causes 200 000 deaths in the Unites States, more than 700 000 hospitalisations, 40 million outpatient visits and 50 million additional illnesses estimated that the present value of economic losses would be USD 550 billion if similar health impacts are extrapolated to all high income countries (Brahmbatt, 2005).

Figure 2.2. **Diffusion of a pandemic through a global transport network**

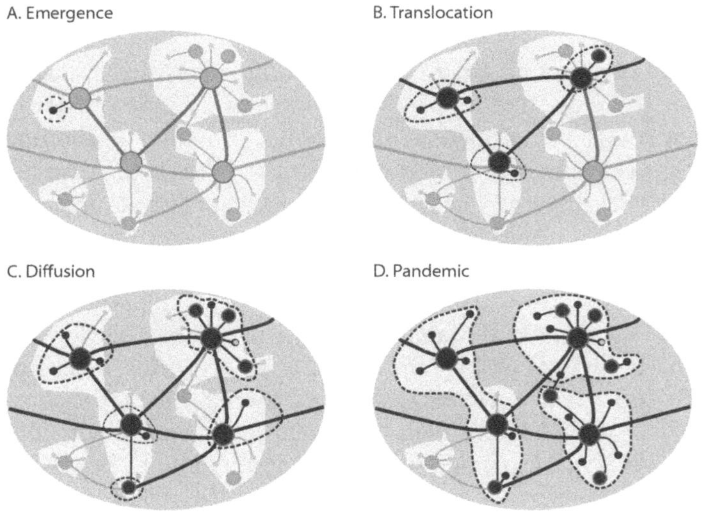

A. Emergence

B. Translocation

C. Diffusion

D. Pandemic

Source: Rodrigue, J.P. (2011), Department of Global Studies and Geography, Hofstra University, copyright © J.P. Rodrigue, available at *http://people.hofstra.edu/geotrans/eng/ch9en/appl9en/diffusionpandemicnetwork.html*.

Comprehensive risk assessments in industrialised economies not only assess the epidemiological features of a virus, they seek to identify populations and geographic areas at risk of epidemics, thereby lending focus to prevention and mitigation efforts. The data also helps to model the trajectory of local outbreaks into global pandemics, which look for a combination of certain social conditions and systems of travel and trade (Rubin, 2010). Population density, for example, is a social condition well correlated with the outbreak of epidemics. Modern air travel means that an outbreak of infectious disease in one country could spread worldwide in a matter of days in the past it would have taken months or years. The 2002 outbreaks of Severe Acute Respiratory Syndrome (SARS) illustrated that one person in the densely populated city of Hong Kong, China could transmit a virus to guests staying in the same hotel, thus enabling the virus to spread quickly worldwide once they returned to their homes in airplanes.

Additional means for local outbreaks to spread globally include animal-to-human transmission. In the case of H5N1 influenza, the so-called avian flu, this reflects migratory bird patterns to some extent, but it also reflects robust, international smuggling activity. H5N1 influenza has yet to mutate to efficiently allow human-to-human transmission, but 15 countries (13 Asian, 2 African) have reported human infections to WHO, accounting for a total of 526 human cases confirmed and 311 deaths (WHO, as of 2 March 2011).

Financial crises

Financial crises encompass a broad variety of situations in which financial institutions or an asset class suddenly lose a large part of their value, *e.g.* bank-runs, financial asset bubble bursts, currency crises, balance of payments crises and sovereign default. The direct results of such events are a loss of paper wealth, but more importantly they may spread to the real economy with the onset of recession due to dependence of consumer demand and business investment on high levels of debt. When lending contracts, debt-fuelled expansion is no longer possible and a sharp economic slowdown becomes inevitable. Rude corrections in the housing market during the latest recession worsened the slowdown in consumer spending as households could no longer borrow against rising equity values. The resulting slowdown of investment in the real economy impacts actors at all levels, from small businesses to home-buyers. Bankruptcies lead to job losses and a drop in aggregate demand, leading to more businesses and individuals being unable to repay their loans, reinforcing a downward spiral that can trigger a recession, depression or bring about stagflation in the real economy. This can have a devastating impact not only on economic prosperity across the board, but also on consumer sentiment and trust in the ability of the system to generate long-term wealth and growth.

Well before the global financial crisis of 2008, regional and national financial crises had increased in number, frequency and severity over the past two decades (*e.g.* in Japan, Mexico, south-east Asia, Russia, Turkey, Argentina). Multiple theories have been put forward about how financial crises develop and how they could be prevented, but there is little consensus since each one is different in important respects. It appears likely that they will continue to occur, which is precisely why tools are needed to anticipate them and reduce the severity of their impacts.

When an overleveraged borrower is a sovereign nation or major financial institution, recent history illustrates how defaults carry the risk of contagion in a globally interconnected economy. In complex systems with network structures like those exhibited by financial institutions, however, shocks can and will emerge endogenously, *i.e.* triggered from within the system itself. It does not necessarily take an major exogenous shock to trigger and maintain the unfolding of a financial crisis and the eventual collapse of the system. Box 2.1 describes the observations of an agent based model using leverage levels for one European country. It observed synchronisation of behaviour amongst actors in the financial system when there is an excessive level of leverage throughout the system.

Box 2.1. **Agent-based models to understand the leverage cycle on national scales**

Using an agent based model in which informed (professional) traders and uninformed (noise) traders observe the same market information (*i.e.* asset prices) and when liquidity began to dry up, they started to behave in similar ways – hence synchronisation. The simulation set the same rules for all agents across the system (such as leverage contracts, lending conditions, margin calls, etc.). Under such conditions, plummeting asset prices rendered banks unable or unwilling to provide credit as they feared they might be unable to cover their own liabilities due to potential loan defaults.In scenarios of high leverage, investors can overload on risky assets, betting more than what they actually have to gamble. Although this is an obviously dangerous practice, it also creates a tremendous level of vulnerability in the system as a whole. Two events in particular can lead to a devastating collapse of a system under the weight of significant levels of leverage:

1. Small, random fluctuations in the demand of an asset by uninformed investors can cause the asset price to fall below its "true value", leading to the development of a "mispricing signal".

2. In order to exploit this opportunity for arbitrage, investment funds capitalise on the maximum allowable leverage level and take massive positions.

If the uninformed traders happen to sell off a bit of the asset and the price drops, the funds stand to lose large amounts of money. This prompts some firms to take even greater amounts of leverage, while other firms may even be forced to begin selling off more of the asset to satisfy their margin requirements. Naturally, this will have the effect of further depressing the price, resulting in a vicious cycle of price drops, greater leverage, and more enforced selling of the asset in reaction to margin calls. Over a short period of time, what seemed like a stable system can cascade into a scenario in which the asset price crashes, causing major losses and bankruptcies by highly leveraged firms. Importantly, only in systems characterised by high levels of leverage can such small changes trigger such catastrophic collapses.

Source: Thurner (2010).

Figure 2.3 represents an actual network of financial institutions (*e.g.* banks and hedge funds) with a few key lenders located at the centre hubs, and many borrowers hovering around the periphery. Two types of network effects can be inferred from this image, both with relevancy for systemic risk in financial markets. First, in the lending relations between leverage providers and leverage takers, one bank is often the source of leverage to a series of hedge funds. If one of these funds comes under stress this might cause the bank to issue margin calls not only to the fund under stress but to all the funds it extends credit to. Second, the asset-liability network between banks becomes relevant if one bank experiences losses or default. This might trigger contagion effects through the banking network, if no exogenous interventions occur (Thurner, 2010). The asset and liability networks of banks in Europe are extremely dense, and can contribute a further layer of systemic risk. When empirically studied for an entire economy, banks have been shown to display a scale-free form of organisation and are consequently highly vulnerable against the shortfall of one of the network's hubs (Thurner, 2010).

Figure 2.4 illustrates such contagion resulting from the mutual ownership and credit relations of banks that can transmit default of debt payments. A recently published simulation of contagion effects and contagion dynamics in banking networks revealed that the most sensitive feature is a bank's degree of "connectedness". This measures a bank's connections to other banks, and at the same time measures how strong those connections are relative to the network's overall assets. Absent intervention by a government or some other financial institution, banks with high "connectedness" can bring lending within the entire banking system to a halt due to consecutive instances of illiquidity (Thurner *et al.*, 2010).

Extrapolating this reasoning to a more macro level, the liberalisation of capital flows has facilitated high integration between international financial markets, increasing interdependence among many economies. Understanding the behaviour of international financial markets' interdependencies is crucial for determining whether contagion effects might occur that can cause systemic risk. Economists often debate whether observing crises in many countries around the same time is truly caused by contagion from one market to another, or whether it is, instead, caused by similar underlying problems that would have affected each country individually even in the absence of international linkages. The 1997 Asian financial crises showed that the interdependence among the financial markets during tranquil periods was different from that of crisis periods, where interdependence was often observed to break down. This break is thought to be due to financial panics or the herding or switches of expectations. Consequently, a strong increase in the co-movements (correlations) of the returns between markets was observed. It is argued by some that a structural break in the correlations demonstrates that the international propagation mechanisms of financial shocks are discontinuous (Morley, 2006).

One of the influential models of credit cycles is an economic model that shows how small shocks to the economy might be amplified by credit restrictions, giving rise to large output fluctuations (Kiyotaki and Moore, 1997). The model assumes that borrowers cannot be forced to repay their debts, therefore, in equilibrium, lending occurs only if it is collateralised. This collateral requirement amplifies business-cycle fluctuations because in a recession, the income from capital falls, causing the price of capital to fall, which makes capital less valuable as collateral, which in turn limits firms' investment by forcing them to reduce their borrowing, and thereby worsens the recession. The model has become influential because earlier real business-cycle models typically relied on large exogenous shocks to account for fluctuations in aggregate output. The Kiyotaki-Moore model shows instead how relatively small shocks might suffice to explain business-cycle fluctuations, if credit markets are imperfect.

Figure 2.3. **A network of financial institutions**

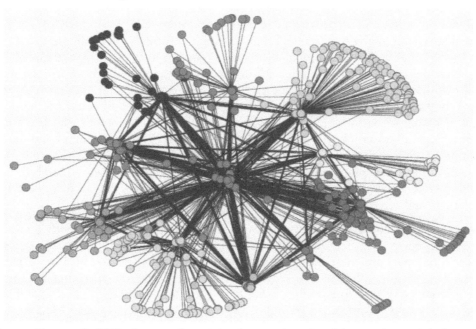

Source: Thurner, S. (2010), *Systemic financial risk: agent-based models to understand the leverage cycle on national scales and its consequences*, OECD, Paris.

Figure 2.4. **Network analysis: a diagram of systemic interbank exposures**

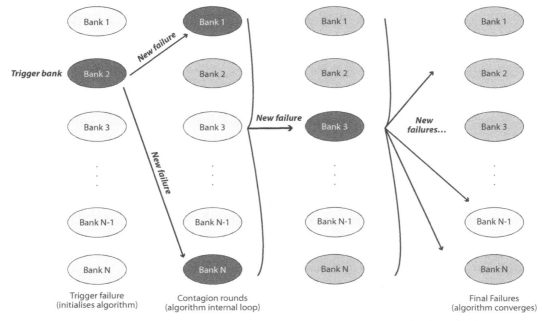

Note: This figure depicts the dynamics of a network analysis. Starting with a matrix of interbank exposures, the analysis consists of simulating shocks to a specific institution (the trigger bank) and tracking the domino effect to other institutions in the network.

Source: IMF (2009), "Global Financial Stability Report, Responding to the Financial Crisis and Measuring Systemic Risks", in *World Economic and Financial Surveys, Global Financial Stability Report, Responding to the Financial Crisis and Measuring Systemic Risks*, International Monetary Fund, Washington, DC, available at *www.imf.org/external/pubs/ft/gfsr/2009/01/pdf/chap2.pdf*, p. 6.

Cyber risks

Although individual cyber-related events can generate a great deal of harm and financial suffering, many experts hold that it is highly unlikely that a single cyber attack currently has the capacity to propagate onwards and become a full-scale global shock (Sommer and Brown, 2010; Riguidel, 2010). Such an attack would have to identify and exploit a hitherto unknown fundamental flaw in the critical technical protocols of the Internet, and arrive under conditions where agreement for remedy could not be quickly reached. Another scenario for a global shock consists in a succession of sustained, multiple zero-day cyber-attacks on key critical infrastructure sectors by perpetrators of great skill, determination and without concern that their actions might result in harm to themselves. A zero-day attack is a computer threat that tries to exploit application vulnerabilities that are unknown to the software developer and vendor, and exploits that security hole before it can be patched.

Several observations underpin the position that a global shock is currently an unlikely result of a cyber attack. The Internet was designed from the start to be robust, so that failures in one part are routed around. In most cyber-events there is no loss of physical resource. Historically, solutions to discovered flaws in software and operating systems and/or the emergence of new forms of malware have been found and made available within a few days. Few single Distributed Denial of Service (DDoS) attacks have lasted more than a day. Many government departments and major businesses and organisations have ICT-related back-up and contingency plans; and many of the networks transmitting the most important data, for example about world financial transactions, are not connected to the Internet, use specialised protocols and equipment, and have reasonably strong levels of access control. Any successful compromise is thought by some experts to require insider knowledge, which argues in favour of better vetting procedures for employees and visitors (Sommer and Brown, 2010).

Under the first scenario mentioned above in which a previously unknown vulnerability in the Internet is exploited, the cyber attack would have to target and disrupt a minimum amount of major hubs in order to propagate to the scale sufficient to compromise the functioning of the entire network. In scale-free networks as large as the Internet there are just enough high-connectivity nodes to keep the network connected under any number of randomly broken nodes. A random breakdown of nodes will leave some highly connected sites intact, and they will keep a large portion of the network connected. An attack that targets about 5% of these highly connected sites, however, has the capacity to make the Internet collapse, very rapidly breaking down the entire network to small, unconnected islands, containing no more than 100 computers each (Cohen *et al.*, 2001). Large scale-free networks are fairly impervious to random node breakdowns, but if large hubs are targeted methodically, even large scale-free networks can be broken up into separate islands (Grubesic and Murray, 2006). Thus, networks like the Internet are resilient to random breakdown of nodes, but very sensitive to intentional attacks on the highest connectivity nodes, such as telecommunication switching centres, because a scale-free network's stability depends on the state of its large hubs.

A more likely scenario for a global shock due to a cyber attack entails a combination of events. Perfect storm conditions could exist should two different cyber-events occur simultaneously, or if a cyber-event were to disrupt critical infrastructure at the same time as some other form of disaster or attack (such as a pandemic or natural disaster that prevents technical experts from defending and patching the system or rerouting capacity from being used). Utilities, such as electricity, gas, water and oil services require constant monitoring of supply systems. Monitoring operations present cyber-vulnerabilities that could be exploited, potentially leading to massive disruption for households, manufacturers, retailers and public services (Sommer and Brown, 2010).

Since the 1960s many industrial control systems have been increasingly monitored and controlled remotely using Supervisory control and data acquisition (SCADA) computing equipment. SCADA are used for the flow of gas and oil through pipes, the processing and distribution of water, the management of the electricity grid, the operation of chemical plants, and the signalling network for railways. More recent systems incorporate load forecasting, adjusting the state of a supply network ahead of actual demand. Earlier SCADA systems were proprietary to specific vendors, but are now moving to an open networked model. Newer industrial control systems communicate using Internet protocols, sometimes over the public Internet to remove the cost of dedicated communications links. Such systems are even more open to cyber attacks than legacy systems, although the vulnerabilities of the latter are also numerous according to experts (Weiss, 2010).

The inability to measure the full disruptive effects of cyber attacks prevents the gathering of compelling evidence that they could amount to a global shock. Firms often conceal that they have been victim of an attack, although this might be apparent in the case of worldwide disruption. Key assumptions distinguish various methodologies for the total cost of a cyber attack. As there is seldom much in the way of direct physical loss, the immediate losses are often limited to the value of destroyed, corrupted or compromised data, costs to replace it, and reputational loss. Some organisations would include remedial costs for the installation of detective, preventative and mitigating technologies as part of the total cost. Whether loss of revenue (based on a previous year's business records) and lost business opportunities should be included in the damages of a cyber attack are debated.

While the frequency of cyber attacks seems to increase nearly every year, only a few instances of malware, worm viruses and Distributed Denial of Service (DDoS) attacks have ever had international impacts, and their severity of disruption was quite limited in duration. Even the most severe attacks rarely rise beyond the level of local harm; there are relatively few instances of cyber attacks that swamp and disable government, banking and newspaper services for several days as was the case in Estonia (2007). Identifying and assessing specific risks related to cyber attacks entail several key differences when compared to natural risks. Earthquakes are bound to happen along a fault, and flood surges are a part of a river system's natural cycle. Where cyber attacks will occur and where they come from is not as straightforward. They result from intentional acts that exploit some vulnerability in code to unlawfully access, steal, destroy or corrupt data. One does not typically know when or if a vulnerable system will be exploited in advance unless warned. For this reason, cybersecurity policy amongst organisations that rely heavily on their ICT systems is to assume that any vulnerability will be exploited and try to identify and patch them first. In addition to firm level assessments, networks of Computer Emergency Response Teams (CERT) and Computer and Computer Security Incident Response Teams (CSIRT) spread knowledge about known vulnerabilities and distribute patches to fix them both at national and international level.

Geomagnetic storms

Large, violent eruptions of plasma and magnetic fields from the Sun's corona, known as coronal mass ejections (CMEs), are the origin of geomagnetic storms (National Academy of Sciences, 2008). Not all CMEs head towards the Earth, but when they do it takes two to three days for its particles to reach and interact with the Earth's geomagnetic field (NERC, 1990). Disturbances in the Earth's geomagnetic field can disrupt the operation of critical infrastructures relying on signals from satellites involved in the Global Positioning System (NAS, 2008, 2009). They can also cause geomagnetically induced currents (GICs) that overload the circuits and trip breakers of terrestrial electrical systems, and in extreme cases melt the windings of heavy-duty transformers, causing permanent damage (NOAA, 2004a). Worldwide manufacturing capacity of high-voltage power transformers is limited to about 70–100 units per year, and thus widespread transformer damage could lead to very long-duration outages in extended geographical areas (Kappenman, 2005).

The most severe space weather event recorded in history is the Carrington Event of 1859, which disrupted telegraph networks and outages around the world as a result of the currents generated. An event of the same magnitude today could be catastrophic, with some damage estimates as high as several trillion dollars (United States House Homeland Security Committee, 2009). The electricity production and distribution infrastructure of modern societies makes them more susceptible to such events. The total length of high-voltage power lines crisscrossing North America has increased nearly tenfold since the 1950s; this has turned power grids into giant antennas for GICs. While the 11-year cycle of geomagnetic disturbances gives some sense about when to expect peak solar activity, the strength of a CME by itself is a poor indicator of whether an ensuing geomagnetic storm will have an effect on terrestrial electric utility systems. Ground conductivity plays an important role, as do the direction of extra high voltage (EHV) lines (Barnes *et al.*, 1991). The assets most likely to be affected are long EHV lines and transformers in more northern latitudes.

Box 2.2. **The Quebec blackout storm**

On 13 March 1989, a geomagnetic storm affected power systems in the United States and Canada. The resulting major power outage lasted for nine hours and covered the majority of Quebec and parts of the northeastern United States (Molinski *et al.*, 2000). The geographic location of Hydro-Quebec grid's and its 1 000 km transmission lines to the load centre made it susceptible to geomagnetic storms (Kappenman and Albertson, 1990). The GICs flowing through the power system severely damaged seven static compensators on the La Grande network in the Hydro-Quebec grid, causing them to trip or shut down automatically before preventive measures were possible (NERC, 1990). The same event caused power losses in central and southern Sweden when GICs disrupted six 130kV power lines (Babayev *et al.*, 2007).

The loss of the compensators in Quebec resulted in a system disturbance and severe equipment damage. Unavailability of new equipment to replace the La Grande network's damaged equipment prevented power restoration to the transmission network. The power delay was also due to the damaged equipment and load transfers at the distribution network level. While work was being conducted to bring power back to the Hydro-Quebec grid, the New Brunswick and Ontario power systems helped provide emergency assistance to Quebec. As power was restored to Hydro-Quebec, it received assistance from New England and New York systems as well as the Alcan and McLaren systems based in Quebec. The voluntary reduction of power use by industrial customers during the incident also helped Quebec to meet its power demands. After nine hours, 83% of full power was restored but one million customers were still without electrical power (NERC, 1990). The total cost of the Hydro-Quebec incidents is estimated to be USD 6 billion. (Canada/OCIPEP, 2002). Since the incident, the Canadian government has set up protective measures at the Hydro-Quebec site, such as transmission line series capacitors, which cost more than $1.2 billion, to block GICs from damaging the system (Canada/OCIPEP, 2002).

Figure 2.5 puts a frequency on severe geomagnetic events over a 22-year solar cycle based on latitude (Molinski, 2000). The probability of occurrence is estimated to range from two-tenths of a percent in northern latitudes to two-thousandths of a percent in the southern regions of the United States. The base line scenario for this study, however, is much weaker than the Carington event or that which caused the 1989 Northeast blackout. By displaying probability and vulnerability geographically, Figure 2.5 provides one approach for urban areas to consider the likelihood of an event. Montreal, Ottawa, Quebec, and Vancouver, for example, fall into regions of low conductivity and in between probability bands of 0.02 and 0.1% of a storm within a 22-year cycle. Boston, New York, and Seattle are also in regions of low conductivity, but within a lower probability band (between 0.02 and 0.009%).

The potential for an extreme geomagnetic storm to produce cascading effects on critical infrastructure raises the need to conduct formal risk assessments in at least two areas. First, there is a need for countries to conduct critical infrastructure dependence exercises determining the cascading effects of the loss of electric power. In addition to providing insight into the consequences stemming from an extreme geomagnetic storm, this form

Figure 2.5. **Probability of a severe geo-electric event occurring over a 22-year solar cycle**

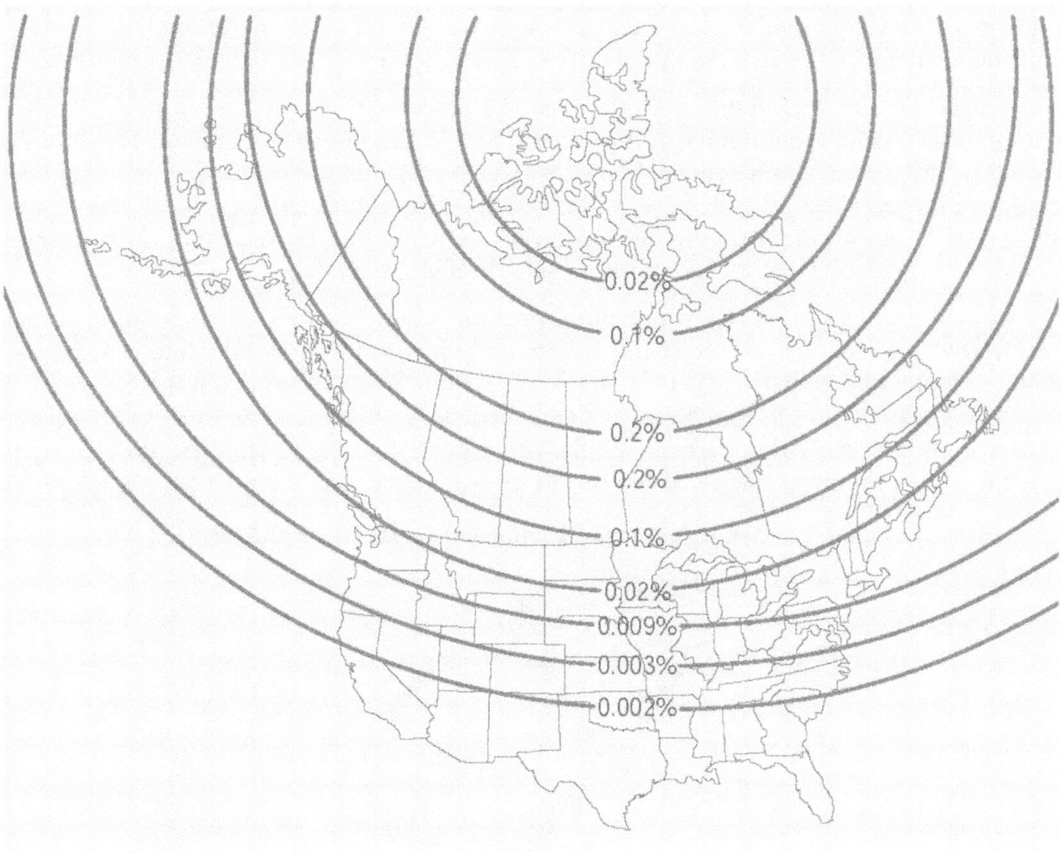

Note: The probability of a geomagnetic storm in which the field change is greater than 300 nanoteslas per minute can be as high as 0.2% per unit time. But the impact of the storm on a power system depends on the earth's local resistivity.

Source: Molinski, T., Feero, W., and Damsky, B. (2000), "Shielding grids from solar storms" in *IEEE Spectrum*, available at *www.engineering.dartmouth.edu/spacescience/wl/res /ae/biblio/molinski00.pdf.*

of risk analysis will also be applicable to other hazards that could interrupt electricity supplies, whether natural or man-made. Second, countries should conduct assessments evaluating their dependence on space-based assets for continuity of government operations. An extreme geomagnetic storm could result in both short- and longer-term disruptions to space-based assets essential to governments for communications, navigation, and information technology.

Lack of knowledge about amplifiers

As an event propagates through a system, it may encounter components known as amplifiers that increase risks for other components in the system. Amplification occurs when such interaction forms a vicious cycle, and thereby reinforces the effects of amplifiers. Figure 2.6 illustrates the point, with an exogenous shock to financial markets (Step #1) that results in falling investment and output (Step #2). This in turn causes lower aggregate demand (Step #3), a decline in asset prices (Step #4) and a tightening of financing conditions (Step #5), which engenders a continued fall in investment and output (a return to Step #2) thereby amplifying the cycle (Korinek, 2009). Amplifiers represent not only mechanisms that boost the scale of a shock to a particular system, but also a means to spread or intensify a hazard throughout several systems. This phenomenon is especially prevalent in concentrated and interdependent systems, and is an increasingly important consideration for policy makers in light of the trends described in Chapter 1 of this report.

Amplifiers are often hubs, or well-connected actors within a system or network, that tend to pass risks on to numerous other actors. In a situation where one actor is responsible for a large share of financing (*e.g.* a very large bank), an intense restriction on lending could substantially amplify the risk in the system. This actor could spread risk in a way substantially out of proportion to its role in the system as the consequences of its restrictions, or the possibility of its failure, propagate through the system.

Identifying the process by which amplification occurs, as well as the conditions that can lead to the creation of amplifiers, is extremely important for conducting risk assessment of potential global shocks. Without clear knowledge of what factors or entities could amplify a local crisis into global shock, decision-making processes and subsequent resource allocations will underestimate the full potential of risks. Amplification played a critical role in the propagation of the recent global financial crisis as weaknesses in the

Figure 2.6. **A simple schematic model of financial amplification**

Source: Adapted from Korinek, A. (2009), "Systemic Risk: Amplification Effects, Externalities, and Policy Responses", in *ONB Working Paper No. 155*, available at *www.oenb.at/en/img/wp155_tcm16-111934.pdf.*

banking sector exacerbated the credit crisis and the bursting of the housing bubble. Many experts classify financial mechanism amplifiers into balance sheet amplifiers (*e.g.* leverage, tight credit conditions, limited capital) and information amplifiers (*e.g.*, opacity, complexity, uncertainty) (Krishnamurthy, 2009). Weaknesses such as excessive leverage, inadequate and low-quality capital and insufficient liquidity buffers in the banking system not only created its own unique struggles, but exacerbated the severity of the financial crisis by a procyclical de-leveraging process and the inter-connectedness of systemically important financial institutions (Basel Committee on Banking Supervision, 2010).

Recently, policy makers in both the United States and European Union have taken steps to prevent similar sets of vulnerability from accelerating future crises. Stress tests, a process whereby a system is subjected to particularly adverse circumstances to identify likely responses and understand a "breaking point" in its normal operation, have been used to assess resilience in the banking sector. Specifically, these tests assess the stability, strength and resilience of a particular entity or system to constraints beyond regular operational norms and provide guidance on areas in need of improvement, restructuring, or rebuilding (Aragones, Blanco, and Dowd, 2001). They are useful in identifying system capacity and limitations. For instance, the recent stress tests in Europe's banking sector aimed at assessing resilience to future shocks worse than that faced by Lehman Brothers Holding, Inc. in 2008, by simulating a double-dip recession and a stock market crash, among other variables (Thomson Reuters, 2010). In these particular tests many banks did not provide full disclosure about the amount of their government debt holdings, when sovereign risk is of great concern to markets (Blundell-Wignall, A. and P. Slovik, 2010). All critical systems, and not just the banking sector, need to design and implement stress tests. Overall, the rationale for companies to use stress testing is to analyse whether their products or services will remain competitive even under new and unfamiliar conditions. By running stress tests through an entire system, and not just its components, policy makers can better identify the relative weak links likely to be affected by a given shock, and focus efforts to prevent potential amplifiers from spreading risks to multiple actors, sectors, or geographical regions.

As amplification occurs within a system, it can create tipping points that make for dramatic, often irreversible, changes. While tipping points are not necessarily negative, it is important to understand where and when they might occur in order to prepare for and/ or attempt to prevent them. For instance, an important role of waste-water treatment is to ensure that the affluent emitted into water sources does not reduce the oxygen saturation of the water below levels suitable for water-based plant or animal life. Since plants in the water contribute to oxygen saturation and water quality, chemicals or other wastes dispersed in the water which kills off plant life act as an amplifier of the negative effect on the system. At the tipping point, the plant life decreases to below a level where it can contribute to improving water quality and oxygen saturation, ultimately affecting the future health of the system and making growth very difficult.

Knowing where, when and how amplification occurs should enable policy to substantially reduce uncertainty during a global shock situation. Once amplifiers are identified, policies can be tailored to act upon these components to maximise the impact of intervention on reducing and/or remedying the problem. In the example of water pollution, a clear understanding of the amplification effects within the ecosystem leads to several actionable conclusions (*e.g.* requiring treatment of the pollutant prior to its release). Likewise, in a banking system, understanding which banks are at risk of collapse and whether or not that collapse would have adverse effects throughout the system, allows action to be focused on the areas of highest vulnerability rather than spreading resources haphazardly across areas that do not present as high a risk.

This knowledge of where the risk of amplification in a system lies also focuses effective monitoring and surveillance systems, which can be used to identify vulnerabilities in a complex system and drive policy action that can reduce the risks associated with amplification. Monitoring potential amplification effects could be a useful policy tool in a wide range of areas including financial institutions at risk of collapse, environmental systems that are being degraded, and both positive and negative social trends.

It is often unknown and difficult to identify or validate exactly what components in a system represent amplifiers. In part this is due to the unavailability of data, which prevents assumptions about the presence of amplifiers from being validated. Populations that act as amplifiers in pandemics, for example, vary according to the characteristics of the virus itself. For the recent H1N1 pandemic, certain healthcare workers and students were thought to represent "super-spreaders", but there are no data to confirm or falsify the hypothesis (Rubin, 2010). Healthcare workers are in near constant contact with infected individuals, while students are often in close quarters with relatively large groups where transmission could occur quickly.

Another challenge in identifying amplifiers lies in a lack of understanding about the system and the interrelation of its components. Knowledge in this area can be improved by advances in mapping and modelling that illuminate the components of a system (see Chapter 3). In some cases the identification of amplifiers is further confounded by a divergence in perception about what constitutes risk. For example, hedge-fund professionals might perceive leverage as a tool to control risk, while their clients view it purely as a risk amplifier (Ineichen, 2009). This difference of perception, especially in the absence of compelling data, adds a qualitative layer to understanding amplification in systems. Social amplifiers such as risk perception, media attention, hazard characteristics, rumour, first responder actions and private citizen/ government trust interact in a dynamic setting (Burns *et al.*, 2007). Obesity trends, for example, are driving the adaptation of services and institutions to increased body-size, thereby reducing some practical difficulties associated with obesity and possibly contributing to the problem (IRGC, 2010).

Accounting for secondary effects

Most assessments of losses from disasters focus on what is often referred to as "direct" impacts, such as property damage, on-site business interruption, or lives lost (Rose, 2009). Identifying and quantifying secondary effects (*e.g.* off-site business interruption, reductions in property values and stock market effects) represent a critical part of a comprehensive risk-management strategy. The indirect nature of these costs does not necessarily make them any less significant in scale or intensity of their impact, indeed the indirect impacts can be even greater than the direct damages. Box 2.3 describes the 2001 foot and mouth outbreak, which illustrates negative secondary effects that resulted from a policy decision in reaction to a crisis.

Destructive forces in a primary system often produce disruptive impacts in adjacent or interdependent systems. Managing such secondary effects requires cataloguing all sectors that the primary system supplies as well as assessing the feasibility of mounting resources to combat such a diverse range of impacts. Uncertainties about causal relations pervade such analysis. Collaboration across jurisdictions and between competitors is therefore often necessary to develop strategies to stem or slow the progression of a global shock or limit its damage at the outset. This requires not only a more expansive mapping approach to fully understand the points of intersection between different sectors of a system, but also greater collaboration to anticipate spillover effects and to co-ordinate a response that maximises available resources.

Box 2.3. **Secondary effects of foot and mouth disease outbreak**

During the 2001 foot and mouth disease outbreak in the United Kingdom, the epidemic's direct impacts were in the agricultural sector via the infection of sheep and cattle populations. These impacts were overshadowed in cost by losses in the tourism industry, an unexpected secondary effect of policies aimed at containing the disease (Irvine, 2005). The Royal Society of Edinburgh released a report claiming: "In formulating policy to deal with a livestock epidemic it is inadequate to treat it as purely an agricultural problem." The same report discusses in detail how the closure of certain tracts of land in the countryside to prevent the spread of the disease to humans, along with the widespread disposal of livestock in these regions, significantly reduced tourism from abroad, a major sector for the generation of national income and employment in Scotland (Royal Society of Edinburgh, 2002). Just as policy decisions to contain the foot and mouth disease should take place in a forum where different stakeholders have a voice, so too should international policy co-ordination take policy coherency into account. Where the benefits of countermeasures designed to reduce primary impacts are outweighed by the negative secondary effects, there is an argument to revise the former.

Not only might the magnitude of secondary impacts be potentially greater than the initial event, they can be extremely wide-ranging if a highly connected hub within a complex system is disrupted. Among the critical infrastructure sectors and sub-sectors likely to experience first-order disruptions as a result of an extreme geomagnetic storm are: communications (satellite and wire-line); energy (electric power); information technology; transport (aviation, mass transit) and transport (pipeline and rail).Disruptions to any one of these three critical infrastructures sectors could drive second-order disruptions to other critical infrastructure sectors. Disruptions to electricity production and distribution in particular would have wide-ranging impacts. The scale of these second-order consequences will vary from country to country, depending on a range of factors such as domestic legislation dictating back-up power requirements for hospitals (Centra, 2011). Figure 2.7 displays the direct and secondary critical infrastructure disruptions, as well as their severity, resulting from an extreme geomagnetic storm. The impacts range in severity from localised degradation (*i.e.* services are available but of reduced quality) to widespread outage (*i.e.* services unavailable), and could affect a diverse range of sectors.

Figure 2.7 also distinguishes impacts to different economic sectors according to the duration of disruption. While some secondary effects occur very quickly and remain stable over time, such as the disruption of telecommunications, others develop slowly and increase over time. The power outage depicted would hold broad consequences for the distribution and provision of drinking water, which requires energy for supply, purification, distribution and treatment both of water and waste water (U.S. Department of Energy, 2010). The severity of disruptions resulting from secondary impacts is seen to increase in intensity as the longevity of the original event increases, which underlines the importance of developing rapid recovery capacity.

Social unrest is an additional secondary impact that could result from risks that have long-lasting effects and impact directly on a population's living conditions (Jovanovic, 2010). At a national level, severe social unrest occurred in Haiti following a cholera outbreak that had, as of 19 November 2010, killed over 1 100 people (Katz, 2010). While the source of the cholera, which had never been documented before in Haiti, is not clear, its spread has been intensified by the squalid living conditions and lack of clean water

Figure 2.7. **Direct and secondary critical infrastructure disruptions**

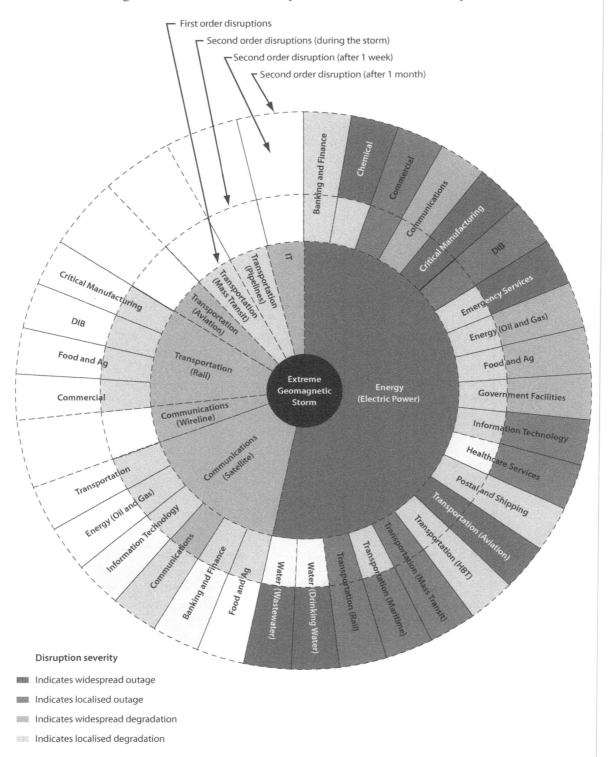

Disruption severity

- Indicates widespread outage
- Indicates localised outage
- Indicates widespread degradation
- Indicates localised degradation

resulting from a magnitude 7.0 earthquake that left more than 300 000 dead and more than 1.2 million homeless (BBC, 2010). The cholera epidemic spurred massive rioting in Haiti that disrupted treatment efforts as well as blocked roads and toppling street lights and electricity transmission lines (Katz, 2010).

Secondary effects eventually become apparent, however indirectly they begin, but there are significant advantages to identifying them as early on as possible. A complete understanding of the scale and intensity of secondary effects facilitates five key actions that are fundamental to the effective management of potential global shocks:

- *Identify policy steps to mitigate the impact of secondary effects:* The most obvious advantage of a complete understanding of secondary effects is its potential to guide policy decisions. The less uncertainty that marks a shock situation, the more reasoned analysis can be brought to bear in advance on the decision-making processes of policy makers and risk managers. This is true before, during, and post-crisis situations all benefit from an understanding of the interdependencies that put other systems at risk. Justifiably, systems at risk of secondary effects are often relegated to a lower priority level, at least initially, to devote more attention to the direct costs of a shock event. Yet these secondary effects can be as large, if not larger, than the direct costs, thus identifying the source of these effects, and their impact deserves attention from the outset of the development of risk management planning.

- *Identify collaborators required in each affected sector:* When additional systems or sectors are affected by secondary effects, a new set of stakeholders and a new set of victims are created, both of whom need to be considered throughout various stages of risk management planning. As dangers arise in adjacent systems, greater collaboration is needed to ensure a holistic response to the shock. Identifying the nature of the secondary effects at play will allow these stakeholders to be more quickly identified, acknowledged and incorporated into the process.

- *Deploy sufficient resources to all sectors likely to be impacted:* Systems or sectors struck by secondary effects are often caught off-guard and unprepared to respond to such indirect sources of risk. Resource allocation decisions surrounded by high levels of uncertainty should be targeted to where they can improve outcomes the most. A thorough knowledge of what secondary effects are likely to emerge will prompt more efficient delivery of human and physical resources to the appropriate sectors as well as facilitate the use of a more efficient strategic response.

- *Pre-emptively develop appropriate contingency plans:* Knowledge of the most likely adjacent sectors to be impacted by secondary effects will allow policy makers and emergency response teams to better prepare for potential outcomes even before the onset of a global shock. It becomes substantially easier to anticipate or respond to a global shock when contingency planning and preparation efforts have already taken root. The greater the visibility policymakers have into probable spillover effects, the better and more efficient responses can be engineered in preparation, more effectively equipping risk managers to mitigate the total cost.

- *Compensate victims in post-crisis period more efficiently:* Without a complete knowledge of all adjacent systems, sectors, and actors affected by the global shock, it is impossible to adequately compensate victims or credibly rebuild what has suffered damage from the shock event. The post-crisis period is one of compensation and rebuilding, increasing the resilience of all affected systems to prevent or mitigate the impact of future crises. Without understanding the landscape of secondary effects, however, it is impossible to appropriately manage the post-crisis process as the basic knowledge of who to compensate and what institutions to strengthen is lacking. The BP oil spill in the Gulf of Mexico had a number of devastating secondary effects, including severely impairing the local commercial fishing industry. As a result, BP developed a compensation plan for local fisherman. As of early July 2010, BP had processed more than 90 000 claims, paying out almost USD140 million (Lee, 2010); a small fraction of the estimated total liability for clean-up and compensation costs for a broad range of claims related to the oil spill. BP itself has estimated this figure to be as high as USD 40 billion.

The likely secondary effects of disruptions to complex systems can be unpredictable, and otherwise extremely difficult to pinpoint. This helps explain why there are still several gaps and shortcomings in current efforts to identify secondary effects and to quantify their economic impacts, despite the importance of doing so. Nonetheless, policies to prevent and mitigate future global shocks will be held to the scrutiny of cost-benefit tests. The benefits are the losses that can be avoided or reduced by such measures, plus any positive spillovers. Loss estimation or impact models are not up to the task, because they are based on data and specifications relating to the normal workings of the economy, rather than crisis situations and the response to them. To estimate total-disaster losses grounded in the principles of benefit-cost analysis policymakers need to identify the various types of loss and major factors affecting them, and establish metrics in accordance with a comprehensive and consistent framework. Professor Rose provides a framework for the analysis and measurement of a disaster's total economic impacts, including an operational definition of resilience social (Rose, 2009).

One of the reasons that identifying these effects can be so difficult is insufficient knowledge and use of mapping techniques. Understanding how complex systems feed into each other, are mutually reinforcing, and display intense interdependencies in times of global shocks, will improve the ability of policy makers and risk managers to anticipate which sectors or systems are likely to experience secondary effects. Additionally, partly due to the fact that these effects can be so hard to identify, there is often a lack of appreciation for the potential scale and intensity of secondary effects. Though the onset of secondary effects can be subtle or hard to pinpoint, their true impact has the potential to be substantial. The secondary effect of foot and mouth disease on the tourism industry in Scotland exceeded that of the cost to the agricultural sector. Finally, secondary and indirect costs of a global shock weaken the political imperative to prioritise the mitigation of these costs. When prioritising response efforts and resource allocation, secondary effects are frequently treated secondarily, yielding to more immediate and visible costs of the global shock at hand.

Outlook for future global shocks

The project on "Future Global Shocks" began in the midst of the financial crises, and as it progressed the world would witness the H1N1 pandemic, the volcanic ash cloud that closed European air space, the BP gulf oil spill, political upheaval in the MENA region, and the Tohoku earthquake and tsunami that led to nuclear accidents at the Fukushima nuclear power plant. Assessing complex systems for vulnerabilities that could transform local risks into global shocks should be an ongoing effort. The drivers and amplifiers that create conditions for potential global shocks are not static, but constantly evolving. Industrialised economies are undergoing significant demographic shifts that hold importance for the social vulnerability of their populations. Climate changes throughout the world require adaptive strategies to deal with environmental risks such as floods, torrential rains, land slides and droughts. Advances in technology, in particular, continue to transform the risk landscape – with healthcare, finance and ICT amongst the strongest economic sectors driving innovation. The benefits of uptake in new technologies are often accompanied by risks of abuse or nefarious 'dual-use' potential. Policy makers in a position to manage these risks contend with critics on one side who accuse them of "Luddite" obstruction while critics on the other side blame them of "Pollyannaism".

Pandemics

Inadequate access to safe water and sanitation, prolonged rainy or dry seasons, and population displacements associated with natural and man-made disasters contribute to the frequency and severity of epidemics. Some of the underlying ecological, environmental and socio-economic changes that aggravate these predisposing drivers are associated with recurring epidemics, but develop outside the purview of health policy controls. For example the increasing number of highly populated and heavily concentrated mega-cities, where weak public health systems and unsanitary living conditions often prevail, is a trend that exacerbates vulnerability factors for pandemics. Most such cities are located in Asia, and focus should especially be given to those few cities where increased international mobility tied to business travel, tourism and migration is common, such as: Manila, Delhi, Mumbai, Kolkata, Chennai and Dhaka. The Pearl River Delta in southern China combines the variables of concentrated economic activity and international mobility that make it stand out in this regard. In addition to being one of the largest manufacturing clusters in the world, the region sees intense trade and business transactions and significant migrations of people from different regions of China as well as networks of people living in different countries. Nearby international transport terminals include Hong Kong, China one of the largest transport hubs in the world (Rodrique, 2011). Due to the influenza virus's incubation period, a flu infection could be transmitted at a Hong Kong airport gateway and diffused rapidly and extensively even before symptoms manifest.

Another underlying driver of epidemics is biodiversity loss, as it appears to function as an important barrier against disease-causing organisms. If the genetic diversity of an affected population is low, invading micro-organisms are more likely to suddenly expand and create epidemic outbreaks with risks of pandemic. Potential pandemics loom as possibilities including those that might be caused by antibiotic-resistant bacteria and known highly infectious agents. The ability of the most dangerous amongst these latter to spread efficiently enough to cause a pandemic is quite limited. Transmission requires close contact with the infected vector, and the vector only has a short time before death or serious illness. A major concern, however, is the technical potential for engineered or synthetic agents to lengthen this time and to lower costs of isolation and stabilisation, which would make their deployment as bio-weapons more feasible (OECD, Royal Society 2010).

Financial risks

As a consequence of fiscal stimulus over 2008-09 and socialisation of part of the private sector's losses, there is now a massive re-leveraging of the public sector. Deficits in excess of 10% of GDP are found in OECD member countries, including the United States, and debt-to-GDP ratios are expected to rise sharply in many cases. Such balance-sheet crises have historically led to economic recoveries that are slow. Sovereign-debt problems are a strong possibility, given the massive re-leveraging of the public sector. In emerging market economies, countries that cannot issue debt in their own currency, or countries that issue debt in their own currency but cannot independently print money (as in the euro area), unsustainable fiscal deficits often lead to a credit crisis, a sovereign default, or other coercive form of public-debt restructuring. In countries that borrow in their own currency and can monetise the public debt, a sovereign debt crisis is unlikely, but monetisation of fiscal deficits can eventually lead to high inflation, which like default is a capital levy on holders of public debt, as it reduces the real value of nominal liabilities at fixed interest rates.

The ongoing sovereign debt problems encountered in Europe are only one dimension of financial risk present in many advanced economies. The dilemma for European countries with fiscal challenges is that, whereas fiscal consolidation is necessary to prevent an unsustainable increase in the spread on sovereign bonds, the short-term effects of raising taxes and cutting government spending tend to cause economic contraction. This complicates the public-debt dynamics and impedes the restoration of public-debt sustainability. In countries that have adopted the euro, if economic growth does not recover, fiscal problems will worsen while making it more politically difficult to enact the reforms needed to restore competitiveness. This might lead to a vicious circle of public-finance deficits, current-account gaps, worsening external-debt dynamics, and stagnating growth. Eventually, this could lead to default on euro-area members' public and foreign debt, as well as exits from the monetary union.

New technologies also present challenges to financial markets, although the risks are not as intuitive as the dual use technologies described above. The sub-prime loan crisis illustrated a break down in the identification, documentation and assessment of risks associated with innovative financial products such as asset backed securities and credit default swaps. More recently, however, modern technological means of trading has begun to take place at such high speed and volume that human or technological error can unintentionally result in extreme volatility. Automated trading in some markets is thought to have played a significant role in so-called "flash crashes" – sudden and extreme drops in financial markets. On 6 May 2010, the Dow Jones Industrials plunged 7% in just 15 minutes.

Box 2.4. High-frequency trading

Many financial institutions have begun to use supercomputers to pick up breaking news, economic information and price and volume movements, to direct automated securities trades in a matter of microseconds – a practice known as high-frequency trading. These supercomputers and algorithms look for signals – such as the movement of interest rates, miniscule economic fluctuations, news and other subtleties – to take advantage of these indications before anyone else in the market is even aware of them. The computer systems being used in the markets today can break down large orders into extremely small slices and execute them across different trading venues at close to the speed of light.

High-frequency traders are phasing out floor-traders and human involvement in an increasingly high volume of trades. Over one-third of United Kingdom equity trading volume is generated through high-frequency automated computer trading while in the United States this figure is closer to three-quarters (UK Foresight, 2011). Research is needed to explore how computer-generated trading in financial markets might evolve in the next ten years, and how this will affect: financial stability; integrity of financial markets including price information and liquidity; competition; market efficiency for allocating capital; transaction costs on access to finance; and the future role and location of capital markets (McGowan, 2010).

Cyber risks

The evolution of cyberspace is too rapid to make predictions, but there seems little prospect that cybersecurity issues will diminish with increasing uptake of ICT throughout the world. The population of Internet users continues to grow, with newer users initially less skilled in computer usage, and hence more vulnerable to security threats. There will be even more computers connected to the Internet, many of which will fail to take basic precautions against falling victim to viruses or allowing their computer to be taken over as a zombie vehicle through which other computers will be attacked. Computer hardware and software will become even more complex and this will make it more difficult to debug flaws (Sommer and Brown, 2010). Marketing and revenue imperatives will continue to prompt vendors to release products with less than exhaustive testing. Businesses and governments will continue to desire the efficiency savings that computerised information systems present and will accelerate the process by which as many transactions with customers, counter-parties and citizens as possible are mediated over the web. As this process goes on, so will the parallel activities of closing down local offices and shedding staff, so that should a web-based service fail, there will be no fail-safe system. At the same time, the cost-savings of just-in-time manufacture and retail distribution will also continue to make use of ICT networks attractive to businesses, as will the opportunities for utility operators to manage large grids of electricity, water and fuel supply via the Internet.

Unless the pace of progress in cyber forensics overtakes the growing ease of deployment and sophistication of deliberate cyber attacks, it will continue to be extremely difficult or victims to ascertain the identity of an attacker – this is the problem of attribution. This means that a defence doctrine based on deterrence is less likely to succeed, and that certain malevolent parties who currently lack the capacity to launch a successful large-scale attack may in future do so. Ever since the advent of the digital economy, there has been a remote risk of massive rejection of the online commercial environment and government services due to lack of trust. Online fraud faces low barriers to entry and will continue to prey on an increasing number of online transactions, which might drive consumers and citizen users away from online transactions and functionality altogether. If business fears over cybersecurity reduce investment in ICT, this could have a significant long-term impact on productivity growth. As Figure 2.8 indicates, ICT has been critical to productivity growth in many

Figure 2.8. **Contribution of ICT capital growth to labour productivity growth in market services, 1995-2004**

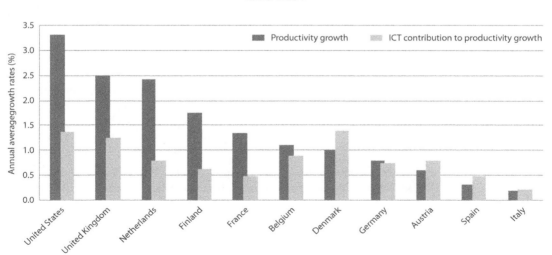

Source: OECD (2008), *The future of the Internet economy: a statistical profile*, OECD, Paris.

countries over the past 25 years. Similarly, consumer cybersecurity fears may impede the transition of many financial and other transactions to much cheaper online platforms. This would represent a significant loss of cost savings to individual businesses and to society of economic efficiency gains and accelerated growth. Finally, new ICT technologies such as the move to "cloud" infrastructures present significant security-relevant opportunities and concerns depending on how they are implemented as described in Box 2.5.

Box 2.5. **Cloud computing – a new variable in the information economy**

Third-party providers are increasingly supplying "cloud computing" storage and computational resources to customers, both private and public organisations alike, through services and underlying infrastructure. The market for these services was estimated at around USD 17 billion in 2009, and is forecast to reach USD 44.2 billion by 2013 (ENISA, 2009). Cloud infrastructures tend to concentrate data and resources, presenting an attractive target to attackers; however they are globally distributed, meaning that confidential data may be held across a number of jurisdictions. Through replication of systems and more robust and scalable operational security they may achieve a level of data redundancy and cybersecurity that would be beyond most smaller-scale enterprises (ENISA, 2009). Customers of cloud services face three main risks associated with off-site data storage. First, external disruptions leading to downtime; second, internal security compromise; and third, access to the cloud via a reliable Internet connection. Cloud services can take measures to prevent or mitigate these risks.

First, external events can lead to disruptions of cloud services. There have been several instances where customers of major cloud-computing companies temporarily lost access to processing capacity and use of essential data services due to power outages at their data centres. To date, these power disruptions have been local, but as discussed above there are possible scenarios for large-scale energy disruptions (*e.g.* geomagnetic storms or a targeted cyber-attack). Firms in the cloud-computing industry have incentive to ensure flawless data security and uninterrupted client access. They need to ensure careful resilience planning, such as fully functional back-up generators and data redundancy via multiple data centres.

Second, cloud services also face internal risks, principally from employees who are in position to compromise large quantities of sensitive data. Industry awareness of this threat is keen, and at least some providers are known to follow a policy of limiting internal access to data by using unique data encryption. With appropriate industry standards and competition between providers, it should also be possible for businesses to manage the day-to-day internal security risks associated with rogue employees.

Finally, if a customer stores essential files and programmes "in the cloud", how will they access these if their Internet service is interrupted? Some vendors offer offline and mobile versions of applications that can be set up to download data daily, weekly or monthly to local machines or simply cache what has been previously accessed for a certain time period. The applications function normally, store changes, and then upload changes the next time the client has Internet access. As long as mobile operators are functional, some cloud service applications offer similar functionality through 3G when Internet Service Providers (ISPs) are down.

Contracts and service level agreements need to include provisions on availability and liability for security breaches, as well as the geographic location of sensitive data and the level of access of third-party staff. Cloud-computing firms and their customers should carefully identify any new interdependencies they create and how they would deal with disruption to essential third-party services such as electricity, telecoms or ISPs.

Source: Adapted from Sommer and Brown (2010).

Conclusions

For a global shock to occur, a set of unusual circumstances have to come together, but the increasing degree of interconnectedness of complex systems in the global economy is making these circumstances more likely to occur.

Gathering information and carrying out risk assessment for global shocks is more complicated than for national disasters taken by themselves, and is likely to require multi-disciplinary expertise. A better understanding is needed of the interconnections and inter-dependencies between different, complex systems to identify potential sources of future global shocks.

There is still much progress needed to estimate total costs of global shocks including secondary effects. The modelling of costs is associated with high uncertainties, and validations are difficult and scarce.

Policy options

With these conclusions in mind, there are steps for risk managers to undertake before any future events actually occur:

- Building and maintaining restricted access models that identify exposed and vulnerable hubs, which if disrupted could lead to a "Global Shock", as well as amplifiers in the system;

- Assessment of the criticality of systems and conditional likelihood of a combination of events that would disrupt the function of hubs; and

- Estimation in monetary terms of the overall, direct and indirect economic consequences of potential shocks. Decision makers also need to take into account how their mitigation and prevention activities might create risks, liabilities or unintended consequences for different parties.

These tasks should be carried out, whenever possible, before weighing options how to prevent and respond to threats, which involves an analysis of costs and benefits in light of an acceptable level of risk.

Bibliography

Ahamad, M. *et al.* (2009), *Emerging Cyber Threats Report for 2009: Data, Mobility and Questions of Responsibility will Drive Cyber Threats in 2009 and Beyond*, Georgia Tech Information Security Center (GTISC), Atlanta.

Ahued-Ortega, A. *et al.* (2010), "Inside the Outbreak of the 2009 Influenza A (H1N1) Virus in Mexico", PLoS One, Vol. 5, No. 10, Zepeda-Lopez *et al.*

Alm, E. *et al.* (2006), *Actuarial Reflections on Pandemic Risk and its Consequences*, European Actuarial Consultative Group, Oxford.

Aragones, J.R., C. Blanco and K. Dowd (2001) "Incorporating Stress Tests into Market Risk Modelling", Institutional Investor Inc., Spring.

Arnold, R. (2006), *A Potential Influenza Pandemic: Possible Macroeconomic Effects and Policy Issues*, Congressional Budget Office, Washington, DC.

Asikainen, T. *et al.* (2010), "Studies needed to address public health challenges of the 2009 H1N1 influenza pandemic: insights from modelling", PLoS Medicine, Vol. 7, No. 6, PubMed, Rockville Pike.

Basel Committee on Banking Supervision (2010), "The Basel Committee's response to the financial crisis: report to the G20", *Bank for International Settlements*.

BBC (2010), "Haiti earthquake: UN seeks record aid donations", *http://news.bbc.co.uk/2/hi/8522732.stm*, accessed 19 November 2010.

Berg, A. *et al.* (2011), "Global Shocks and their Impact on Low-Income Countries: Lessons from the Global Financial Crisis", Research Department, and Strategy, Policy, and Review Department, IMF Working Papers, Washington, DC.

Bickis, M., and U. Bickis (2007), *Predicting the Next Pandemic: An Exercise in Imprecise Hazards*, 5th International Symposium on Imprecise Probability: Theories and Applications, Prague, Czech Republic.

Blundell-Wignall, A. and P. Slovik (2010), "The EU Stress Test and Sovereign Debt Exposures", OECD Working Papers on Finance, Insurance and Private Pensions, No. 4, OECD Financial Affairs Division, www.oecd.org/daf/fin

Bordo M.D., D. Hargreaves and M. Kida (2010), "Global Shocks, Economic Growth and Financial Crises", NBER Working Papers, No. 16 027, National Bureau of Economic Research, Cambridge.

Borg, S. (2005), *Economically Complex Cyberattacks*, the IEEE Computer Society.

Brahmbhatt, M. (2005), *Avian and Human Pandemic Influenza: Economic and Social Impacts*, WHO, Geneva.

Cashell, B. *et al.* (2004), *The Economic Impact of Cyber-Attacks*, CRS Report for Congress, Washington, DC.

CENTRA Technology (2010), *Future Global Shocks Case Study: Geomagnetic Storms*, OECD, Paris.

Coccia, M. (2009), "Business cycles and the scale of economic shock", Ceris Working Papers, Institute for Economic Research on Firms and Growth, Moncalière.

Cookson, C. (2011), "Scientists warn of $2,000bn solar 'Katrina' in Washington", 20 February, *Financial Times Limited*, London.

Deng, Y. *et al.* (2010), "Estimates of the True Number of Cases of Pandemic (H1N1) 2009, Beijing, China", *EID Journal*, Vol. 16, No. 11, *www.cdc.gov/eid/content/16/11/1786.htm*.

Diekmann, N. *et al.* (2008), *CRO briefing: Emerging Risks Initiative – Position Paper*, Critical Information Infrastructure, Amstelveen, November.

Dixon, P., B. Lee and T. Muehlenbeck *et al.* (2010) "Effects on the U.S. of an H1N1 Epidemic: Analysis with a Quarterly CGE Model", *Journal of Homeland Security and Emergency Management*: Vol. 7, Issue 1, Article 75, available at: *www.bepress.com/jhsem/vol7/iss1/75*.

Equity Research (2010), "Swine Flu: Economic Implications", *http://equity-research.com/swine-flu-economic-implications*.

Falagas, M.E. *et al.* (2010), *Epidemiological Aspects of 2009 H1N1 Influenza: the Accumulating Experience from the Northern Hemisphere*, European Journal of Clinical Microbiology & Infectious Diseases, Vol. 29, No. 11.

Fauci, A.S. (2010), *Pandemic Influenza's 500th Anniversary*, National Institute of Allergy and Infectious Diseases, Maryland.

Frey, B.S., and S. Luechinger (2005), "Measuring Terrorism", Working Papers, Number 171, in Alain Marciano and Jean-Michel Josselin (eds.), *Law and the State: A Political Economy Approach*, Cheltenham, UK, and Northampton, MA, USA, Edward Elgar, pp. 142-181.

Fry, R. (2010), "Fighting Wars in Cyberspace", *The Wall Street Journal*, 21 July, Dow Jones and Company, New York.

Frison-Roche, M.A. (2005) (ed.), *Les Risques de Régulation*, Presses de Sciences Po et Dalloz, Paris.

Grubesic, Tony H. and Alan T. Murray (2006) "Vital Nodes, Interconnected Infrastructures, and the Geographies of Network Survivability", *Annals of the Association of American Geographers*, Vol. 96, No. 1, Routledge, London, pp.64-83.

Hapgood, M. (2010), *Space Weather: Its Impact on Earth and Implications for Business*, Lloyd's 360 Risk Insight, Lloyds, London.

IMF (International Monetary Fund) (2006), *The Global Economic and Financial Impact of an Avian Flu Pandemic and the Role of the IMF, the Avian Flu Working Group 1*, Washington, DC.

Ineichen, A. (2009), UBS Hedge Fund Report 2009, available at *www.sfcscapital.com/media/alexander-ineichen-ubs-hedge-fund-report-2009?page=2*, accessed 17 November 2010.

Information Sciences Institute of the University of California (2009), *Report on National Cyber Defense Initiative Industry Workshop*, ISI, California.

IRGC (2010), *Emerging Risks: The Obesity Epidemic*, available at *www.irgc.org/IMG/pdf/ Emerging_risks_Obesity.pdf*, accessed 19 November 2010.

Irvine, W. (2005) "The Impacts of Foot and Mouth Disease on a Peripheral Tourism Area: the Role and Effect of Crisis Management", *Journal of Travel and Tourism Marketing*, Haworth Press.

Jarquin, V.G. *et al.* (2009), "Effect of School Closure from Pandemic (H1N1)", *Emerging Infectious Diseases Journal*, Vol. 17, No. 4, April 2011, Chicago, *www.cdc.gov/eid/content/17/4/pdfs/10-0906.pdf*, accessed 29 March 2011.

Jovanovic, A., O. Renn and R. Schröter (2011), *Social Unrest*, OECD Project on Future Global Shocks, OECD, Paris.

Kamigaki, T. and H. Oshintani (2010), "Influenza Pandemic Preparedness and Severity Assessment of Pandemic (H1N1) 2009 in South-east Asia", *Public Health*, No. 124, Elsevier, pp. 5-9.

Kappenman J (2005) "Too important to fail", *Space Weather* Vol. 3, No.5.

Katz, J. (2010), "Violent Cholera Protests Spread to Haiti's Capital", *Washington Post*, November 19.

Kiyotaki, N., and J. Moore (1997), "Credit Cycles", *Journal of Political Economy*, Vol. 105, No.2, pp.211-248, April 1997, Chicago.

Korinek, A. (2009), *Systemic Risk: Amplification Effects, Externalities, and Policy Responses*, Working Paper 155, Oesterreichische Nationalbank, Austria *www.oenb.at/ en/img/wp155_tcm16-111934.pdf*, accessed 15 November 2010.

Lee, R.C. (2010) "Fishermen caught in a quandary", *Houston Chronicle*, 4 July.

Lewis, J.A. (2002), *Assessing the Risks of Cyber Terrorism, Cyber War and Other Cyber Threats*, Center for Strategic and International Studies, Washington, DC.

Lewis, J.A. (2006), *Cybersecurity and Critical Infrastructure Protection*, Center for Strategic and International Studies, Washington, DC.

Lorenz, J. *et al.* (2009), "Systemic risk in a unifying framework for cascading processes on networks", The European Physical Journal, vol. 71, pp. 441-460, Springer.

May, R., S. Levin, and G. Sugihara (2008), *Complex Systems: Ecology for bankers*, Nature 451, pp. 893-895.

McGowan, Michael. J. (2010), "The Rise of Computerized High Frequency Trading: Use and Controversy", *Duke Law & Technology Review*, *www.law.duke.edu/journals/dltr/ articles/pdf/2010dltr016.pdf*, accessed 21 March 2011.

Molinski, Tom S. *et al.* (2000), "Shielding Grids from Solar Storms," *IEEE Spectrum*, November 2000.

Morley, J. *et al.* (2006), "Detecting Shift Contagion in Currency and Bond Market", *Journal of International Economics*, Vol. 68, No. 2, Elsevier, pp. 409-423.

NAS (National Academy of Sciences) (2008), *Severe Space Weather Events – Understanding Societal and Economic Impacts Workshop Report*, National Academies Press, Washington, DC.

NAS (National Academy of Sciences) (2009), *Severe Space Weather Event Understanding Societal and Economic Impacts: A Workshop Report – Extended Summary*, National Academies Press, Washington, DC.

NERC (North American Electric Reliability Corporation) (1990), *March 13, 1989 Geomagnetic Disturbance*, NERC, Princeton, New Jersey.

NOAA (2004a), *Intense Space Weather Storms October 19-November 7, 2003*, Government Printing Office, Washington, DC.

OECD, Royal Society (2010), *Synthesis Report*, Symposium on Opportunities and Challenges in the Emerging Field of Synthetic Biology, *www.oecd.org/dataoecd/23/49/45144066.pdf*, accessed 18 November 2010.

Overby, S. (2009), "The 25 Most Dangerous Cities for Offshore Outsourcing", *www.csoonline.com/article/482477/the-25-most-dangerous-cities-for-offshore-outsourcing.*

Özlalea, U. and K. Metin-Özcanb (2007), *An alternative method to measure the likelihood of a financial crisis in an emerging market*, Elsevier B.V., Netherlands.

Pfleeger, S.L. and R. Rue (2008), "Cybersecurity Economic Issues: Clearing the Path to Good Practice", IEEE Software, pp. 35-42.

Powner, D. (2009), "National Cybersecurity Strategy: Key Improvements are Needed to Strengthen the Nation's Posture", United States Government Accountability Office, Washington, DC.

National Security Telecommunications Advisory Committee (NSTAC) (2003), *Vulnerabilities Task Force Report: Concentration of Assets: Telecom Hotels*, NSTAC, Washington, DC.

Reinberg, S. (2009), "Pandemic H1N1 Flu Hit Kids Hard in 2009", *HealthDay Reporter*, HealthDay, Norwalk.

Reuters (2011), "Icelandic volcano set to erupt", *www.telegraph.co.uk/news/worldnews/europe/iceland/8311924/Icelandic-volcano-set-to-erupt.html.*

Riguidel, M. (2003), "Les infrastructures critiques et leurs interdépendances : Les systèmes critiques face aux malveillances" (Critical infrastructures and interdependencies), *Revue de l'électricité et de l'électronique* (REE), No. 8, Paris, pp. 73-78.

Riguidel, M. (2008), « Les technologies numériques du futur : Nouvelles menaces, nouvelles vulnérabilités », Cahiers de la sécurité, No. 6, Institut d'Etudes Politiques de Lyon, Lyon.

Rodrigue, J-P *et al.* (2009) *The Geography of Transport Systems*, Hofstra University, Department of Global Studies & Geography, accessed 5 November 2010, *http://people.hofstra.edu/geotrans.*

Rollins, J. and C. Wilson (2007), "Terrorist capabilities for Cyberattack: Overview and policy issues", Congressional Research Service (CRS) Report for Congress, Washington, DC.

Rose, A.Z. (2009) "A Framework for Analyzing the Total Economic Impacts of Terrorist Attacks and Natural Disasters", Journal *of Homeland Security and Emergency Management*, Vol. 6, No. 1, Berkeley Electronic Press, Berkeley.

Royal Society of Edinburgh (2002). "Inquiry into Foot and Mouth Disease in Scotland", July, Edinburgh.

Rubin, H. (2010), "Future Global Shocks: Pandemics", OECD, Paris.

Saxton, F. (2009), "The Aurora Power Grid Vulnerability", *A White Paper*, No Network is 100% Secure series, Easyrider LAN Pro, Oregon.

Smith, G. (2010) "Y2K: crisis averted or con?", *The Irish Times*, 1 January, Dublin.

Sommer, P. and I. Brown (2010), "Reducing Systemic Cybersecurity Risk", OECD, Paris.

The Avian Flu Working Group (2006), *The Global Economic and Financial Impact of an Avian Flu Pandemic and the Role of the IMF*, IMF, Washington, DC.

The Government Accountability Office (GAO) (2010), "Cybersecurity: Key Challenges Need to be Addressed to Improve Research and Development", GAO, Washington, DC.

Thurner, S. (2010), "Agent-Based Models: Understanding the Leverage Cycle on National Scales", OECD, Paris.

Thurner, S. *et al.* (2010) "Leverage Causes Fat Tails and Clustered Volatility", Cowles Foundation Discussion Papers 1745.

United States Department of Energy (2006), "Energy Demands on Water Resources: Report to Congress on the Interdependency of Energy and Water", USDOE, Washington, DC.

United States House of Representatives, Homeland Security Committee, Subcommittee on Emerging Threats, Cybersecurity, and Science and Technology (2009), Statement Prepared by Dr. William Radasky and Mr. John Kappenman, 111th Cong., 2nd sess., 21 July 2009.

Wegener, H. (2007), "Qui se charge de maîtriser les dangers du cyberespace ?", Forum du désarmement: les technologies de l'information et la sécurité internationale, No. 3, Institut des Nations Unies pour la recherche sur le désarmement (UNIDIR), Genève.

Wilkinson, A. (2009), *The Oxford Scenarios: Beyond the Financial Crisis*, The Institute for Science, Innovation and Society, Oxford.

Wilshusen, G.C. (2010), "Cybersecurity: Continued Attention is Needed to Protect Federal Information Systems from Evolving Threats", GAO, Washington, DC.

Chapter 3

Tools to prepare for future global shocks

Most systems that involve multiple interactions by humans and their various activities are inherently complex. These systems are at the heart of future global shocks and, as a result, merit the increased attention of policy makers. Advances in information and communication technology have enhanced the capacity of a new generation of mapping and modelling tools to demystify complex systems, by helping to anticipate, prevent and mitigate adverse extreme events. This chapter describes the need for and utility of such tools as risk maps and threat models to improve situation awareness and support decision making at the planning and operational levels. Mapping and modelling techniques applied to complex systems have made important progress, but their accuracy and predictive power face limitations, some of which could be improved upon with changes to public policy. Even with greater access to data and information, they will require continued refinement to translate results into actionable and effective policies and interventions.

Introduction

Mapping complex systems is useful to identify the hubs that are most likely to serve as the propagation pathways for large-scale disruptions to economic activity. Computerised simulation models can help understand what conditions and variables make an event more likely to result in propagation effects. Together these tools improve the ability of policy makers to conceptualise where to reinforce the weakest of vulnerable points, where to prioritise limited resources and when to centralise, diversify or create redundancy in complex systems.

Mapping and modelling of complex systems

A key characteristic of future global shocks is the propensity of their effects to propagate through complex systems, which are the most likely to produce wide-ranging and long-lasting secondary consequences that may have little to do with an event's initial trigger. Taken together, such knock-on effects may well outweigh the consequences of the initial disruptive event. Figure 3.1 provides a very simplified diagram of an electricity and water distribution system. The power plant at the left of the figure provides electricity to a network of transmission lines. The electricity is then distributed to various customers including businesses, residences and public utilities – such as the water-pumping station that then supplies water to the same customers as the power plant. All of these components together make up a system, as they are all linked to each other in some way – spatially or otherwise.

In Figure 3.2, the same simplified system is displayed, but the power plant has been taken offline. This may occur for any of a variety of reasons, such as a mechanical malfunction or another form of disruptive event (*e.g.* a fire or earthquake). The effects of the loss of power propagate through the system with some components being affected while others are not. In many cases the severity of the impact depends on the longevity of the event (the power outage) and the criticality of the specific components adversely affected.

Figure 3.1. **A simplified electricity and water distribution system**

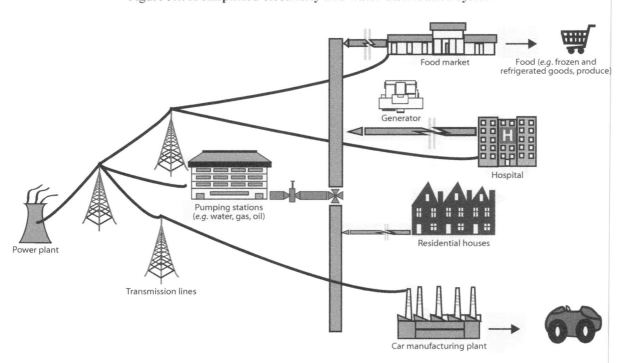

A loss of power at the food market might shut down cash registers making it difficult to conduct business, and it might even lose perishable goods from lack of refrigeration. The car manufacturing plant also relies on electricity for producing output and conducting business operations. The hospital shown in Figures 3.1 and 3.2 is equipped with a generator to provide a back-up supply of electricity. This ensures that short term disruptions to the main supplier do not jeopardise the lives of patients on life support for example; a disproportionately adverse effect to the cost of a reliable generator.

A sustained loss of electricity could create far more severe consequences for the components depicted in Figure 3.2. For instance, sanitation problems in housing units could ensue if water pumping stations lack sufficient back-up power to supply fresh water to residents. The hospital's generator requires fuel, but a long term electricity disruption might impede delivery systems. This could require the prioritisation of medical services, resulting in backlogs where some patients are left untreated.

Even in this very simple system, there are numerous variables – and interactions between the variables – to consider in understanding the extent of the impacts of an event. The initial loss of electricity results in a variety of knock-on effects that follow from, but may only be loosely related to, the initial event. In relatively simple systems – where there are only a few elements and their relationships and interconnections are well understood – it is relatively easy to determine how an event will propagate. This is not the case in complex systems. Indeed it can be very difficult to understand propagation in complex systems because they are: "composed of many parts that interact with and adapt to each other and, in so doing, affect their own individual environments and, hence, their own futures. The combined system-level behaviour arises from the interactions of parts that are, in turn, influenced by the overall state of the system. Global patterns emerge from the autonomous but interdependent mutual adjustments of the components" (OECD GSF, 2009).

Figure 3.2. **Propagation effects of disruption to electricity supply**

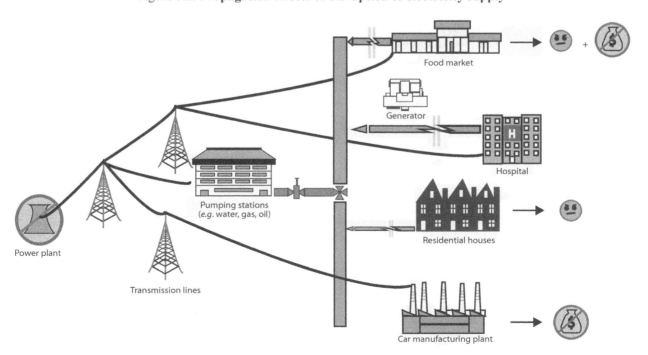

Complex systems are found both in natural systems (*e.g.* the human brain) and man-made systems (*e.g.* the financial system). Understanding key characteristics of complex systems is important for anticipating events that may require policy interventions and identifying where those interventions should or could occur for maximum efficiency. For example, if the water pipes connecting end-users to the pumping station in Figure 3.2 are vulnerable to seismic tremors, one policy option would be to reinforce their robustness. Investments in such an undertaking need to be weighed against, or even added to, the costs of maintaining sufficient surplus in reservoirs and diversified means of distribution should water mains break due to an earthquake.

Box 3.1. **Characteristics of complex systems**

Complex systems can have some or all of the following characteristics, several of which overlap:

- **Adaptability** – elements of complex systems adapt to the action of other components and to changes in their environment.

- **Emergence** – system-level patterns that are not easily identified by examining the system's individual constituents.

- **Self-organisation** – at a system level, the autonomous adaptation to changing conditions as a result of the adaptability of the individual components.

- **Attractors** – a recognisable dynamic state of a system that may continuously reappear.

- **Self-organised criticality** – a self-organising attractor state with an inherent potential to engender abrupt transitions.

- **Chaos** – extreme sensitivity to the initial conditions of the system. Not fully predictable, chaotic systems may nevertheless exhibit order due to an attractor (see above).

- **Non-linearity** – a system in which changes in one property or component may have a disproportionately large effect on another property or component. Prediction in such a system requires sophisticated probabilistic algorithms.

- **Phase transitions** – a system's behaviour may change radically, and sometimes irreversibly, when a certain "tipping point" or phase transition point is reached.

- **Power laws** –When the frequency of an event varies as a power of some attribute of that event (*e.g.* its size), the frequency is said to follow a power law.

Source: OECD Global Science Forum (2009).

Mapping complex systems

A major challenge in analysing future global shocks is the need to understand the way in which any system's various components are interrelated. Maps help identify and quantify the relationship of a system's components. Maps of complex systems are often hard to come by for three principle reasons. First, the complexity of the systems makes mapping difficult. This is sometimes due to the sheer number of components and interconnections, but can also result from a lack of knowledge about key components and connections. Second, understanding a complex system requires detailed knowledge of its component's functions and their interrelations. As each component on its own could be complex, and understanding the various components could individually require specialised skills, developing a map often requires a large interdisciplinary effort. Finally, mapping complex systems requires a sustained effort since they evolve over time. Maps need to be revisited and revised to provide an accurate image of the system.

In addition to traditional, geographic maps there are several types of maps that provide a conceptual system for understanding networks, processes and organisational features.*

- Physical maps delineate the spatial relationships between variables which may be as diverse as national boundaries, population distributions, store locations, or topographical features. These physical maps are highly relevant to risk management, particularly when it comes to physical events, such as natural disasters. For instance, they can be used in the development of response plans and to improve the allocation of emergency management resources.

- Conceptual maps are less common used, but can be used to explain complex systems that may or may not have tangible, physical components. These maps are often helpful in describing "human" networks or other large, complex systems that do not necessarily have an important physical component. Examples of systems that require this conceptual mapping framework include the Internet and social networking (in any form). Complex systems display power-law distributions, where, for instance, Internet traffic is not evenly distributed across websites, but rather several websites account for a disproportionate share of overall Internet traffic.

- Conceptual maps can be particularly useful in illuminating the scope, structure, and evolution of complex systems. What this type of information lacks in actionable data, it makes up for in clarifying a theoretical approach to a new problem and is particularly useful in assessing the potential for the propagation of a hazard and knock-on effects.

- Process or organisational maps describe a sequential and often, but not always, time-dependent process. In practice, these maps can take the form of decision trees, propagation trajectories, an order of operations, an organisational chart or hierarchy, or a description of a domino effect. Process maps offer information on the order or structure of the system (*e.g.* to what extent is it linear?), the options available at each point affect the decision, the various external factors which affect the progression, and finally, a definition of what the outcome or end-result of the system looks like.

To improve the understanding of complex systems, maps need to identify critical elements and the interactions between various elements within the system, such as interdependencies, nodes, hubs, scope, pathways, external factors and gaps. Descriptions of these elements are provided in the report's Glossary. Depending on the need at hand, a single type of map can suffice to aid conceptual understanding of a complex system. In the electricity example above, the geographic location of the various components in the system does not reveal much about their interdependencies, whereas a conceptual map describing the linkages within the electricity system would be useful to asking the right questions and can lead to actionable information. For example, what are the energy sources for electricity generation within the system's scope? What structures and activities rely on the electricity being provided? Where are the back-up facilities and how/where could they be set up quickly in the event of a prolonged blackout? Table 3.1 is a dependency matrix for critical infrastructures (CI) that begins to answer some of these questions. It identifies the degree of dependencies between critical infrastructure sectors by ranking them as high, medium or

---

* See *OECD Future Global Shocks Toolkit*, which discusses in detail different types of maps and their unique advantages.

low. It depicts, for example, water purification as highly dependent upon electrical power, whereas the oil and gas industries, although often thought of as closely linked, are not strongly dependent on one another.

Table 3.1. **Sample dependency matrix**

Sector		Energy and utilities					Services		
Element		Electrical power	Water purification	Sewage treatment	Natural gas	Oil industry	Customs and immigration	Hospitals and health care	Food industry
Energy and Utilities	Electrical power	-	L	N/A	N/A	M	N/A	N/A	N/A
	Water purification	H	-	N/A	N/A	M	N/A	N/A	N/A
	Sewage treatment	L	H	-		H	N/A	N/A	N/A
	Natural gas	M	N/A	N/A	-	L	N/A	N/A	N/A
	Oil industry	H	L	N/A	N/A	-	N/A	N/A	N/A
Oil industry	Customs and immigration	H	L	L	L	L	-	L	N/A
	Hospitals and health care	H	H	L	H	H	M	-	H
	Food industry	H	H	H	L	M	M	L	-

Key: **H** = High; **M** = Medium; **L** = Low.

Source: Pederson *et al.* (2006), Critical Infrastructure Interdependency Modelling: A Survey of U.S. and International Research, Idaho National Laboratory, Idaho, August, available at *http:// cipbook.infracritical.com/book3/chapter2/ch2ref2a.pdf.*

There are five types of interdependence found in critical infrastructures (Pederson *et al.,* 2006):

1. Physical – reliance, often of an engineering type, between components;

2. Informational – information (transfer) or control requirement between components (*e.g.* SCADA systems monitoring and controlling a power grid);

3. Geospatial – relationship of proximity (*e.g.* all assets in a single building could be affected by fire);

4. Policy/procedural – interdependency caused by a policy or procedure that relates components in a system (*e.g.* grounding air traffic after an attack on a plane);

5. Societal – the affect that a component of the system may have on public opinion, fear, confidence, etc. This may be time-sensitive and decay or grow with time (*e.g.* use of a certain infrastructure or mode of transport may fall after a terrorist attack, but return to average levels over time.

Geographic maps of complex systems are unlikely to be readable if they feature too many components. The Internet is a complex system with innumerable connections between pieces of hardware and software situated all over the globe. Researchers have begun mapping the interconnections of the Internet by using distributed programs (on approximately 5 000 computers worldwide) that search out a path to another point on the Internet every few minutes.

Using this data, the conceptual map in Figure 3.3 was produced to explore the functional organisation of the internet (*i.e.* the importance of certain nodes), not simply the number of connections. This shows three distinct sets of nodes in the Internet. The first is a dense core of 100 or so critical nodes that have a large number of connections to other nodes and form the "nucleus" of the Internet. The second set lies outside of the nucleus and is composed of approximately 5 000 isolated nodes that are extremely dependent on the critical nodes in the nucleus as they have few if any other connections. In between these two sets of nodes is the final category composed of around 15 000 peer-connected nodes that are self-sufficient.

Mapping a complex system might require a combined approach. Critical infrastructures, for example, have both important geographical and conceptual components. The geographical component provides essential information about the location of various assets as well as their spatial relationships. As some elements of critical infrastructures are physically and geospatially interdependent, this provides information about the time required to accomplish certain tasks, such as providing raw materials to manufacturing plants or delivering fuel for electricity production or protecting the assets at risk from a natural disaster. The interdependencies in modern critical infrastructure, however, go deeper than simple physical and geospatial links. There are also informational and policy interdependencies

Figure 3.3. **A schematic plot of the Internet in three components**

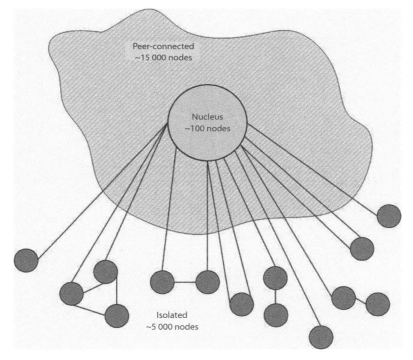

Note: This map of the Internet provides some interesting conclusions regarding the structure of the network and its robustness to disruption. While the core nodes are important, if they are removed, only about 30% of the isolated nodes become entirely isolated from the system. "The remaining 70% can continue communicating because the middle region has enough peer-connected nodes to bypass the core", the number of links required to complete the data transfer simply increases from about 4 or 5 to 8 or 10 (Graham-Rowe, 2007).

Source: Carmi S. *et al.* (2007), "A model of Internet topology using k-shell decomposition", in *Proceedings of the National Academies of Sciences of the United States of America*, Vol. 104, No. 27, pp. 1 1150-1 1154.

that represent key components of the system. Understanding these aspects of the system requires a conceptual map such as Figure 3.4. Physical interdependencies are included such as the provision of cooling water to the production of electricity and natural gas, or the distribution of electricity to the different infrastructure sectors. Figure 3.4 also shows linkages that would have been impossible to present adequately on a geographical map. For example, the finance and banking system provides operating cash for continuous operation in the other sectors.

There are a number of ways that information about a system can be collected to create a map. Primarily theoretical tools, such as scenarios and network analyses, can be used to depict the structure of a system and draw out the interconnections between its various components. The complexity of some systems requires that technological tools be used to collect, distil, and analyse the data necessary to create a map. Geographic Information Systems (GIS) are an important tool that "integrates hardware, software and data for capturing, managing, analysing, and displaying all forms of geographically referenced information", to facilitate visualisation, analysis and interpretation of data to reveal relationships, patterns, and trends (ESRI, n.d.). GIS has been used to analyse systems in a wide range of sectors of

Figure 3.4. **An example of a critical infrastructure interdependencies map**

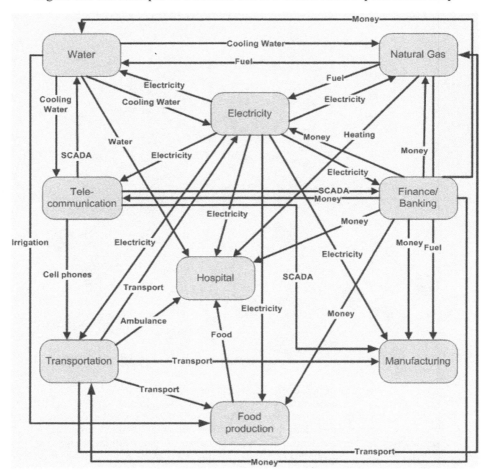

Source: Based on Chai, C.L. *et al.* (2008), "Social network analysis of the vulnerabilities of interdependent critical infrastructures", *International Journal of Critical Infrastructures*, Vol. 4, No 3, pp. 256-273.

activity such as defence and intelligence, business localisation, ecosystem monitoring, natural resource management, and utilities networks. Box 3.2 provides examples of how GIS is used in maritime safety and environmental resources management and protection.

As there are generally a very large number of components within complex systems, networked computing can also be a useful tool in mapping. In the research on mapping the Internet, discussed above, 20 000 computers were enlisted to generate the data required to produce the map (Dimes, 2009). Practically, this means that computer users across the world downloaded a small programme that measured the "distance" from the computer to another point on the Internet. The information was then reported to a centralised station

---

Box 3.2. **GIS for maritime safety and environmental resources management and protection**

In the United States and Europe environmental disasters motivated comprehensive efforts to monitor and protect maritime traffic and to prevent and detect pollution by ships. Both the European Maritime Safety Agency and California Office of Spill Prevention & Response (OSPR) use Geographic Information Systems (GIS) to model vessel traffic patterns and propose potential changes to reduce environmental threats.

In 1989, the Exxon Valdez oil tanker suffered a disastrous grounding and dumped more than 260 000 barrels of oil into a habitat populated by seals, salmon and other wildlife species. The remote location of the Exxon Valdez spill complicated clean-up efforts, and intensified the negative effect on local wildlife populations. In response, the state of California created OSPR and charged it with protecting the state's fish and wildlife against man-made ecological disasters. OSPR developed a GIS system that incorporates multiple data sources, including state-wide infrastructure layers, coastal and marine resources, topographical maps, nautical charts, an environmental sensitivity index, area contingency plans, shipping routes and pipeline plans. Combined with GPS-equipped mobile devices and imaging systems in the field to assist in crisis management, the various components of the system are used to populate an incident database as part of the Natural Resource Damage Assessment (NRDA).

In 1999 the oil tanker Erika broke apart in a storm off the Atlantic coast of France, spilling over 10 000 tonnes of heavy fuel oil, and polluting 400 kilometres of coastline. Following this the European Union established a community vessel traffic monitoring and information system called SafeSeaNet (SSN). SSN enables the receipt, storage, retrieval and exchange of information for the purpose of maritime safety, port and maritime security, marine environment protection and the efficiency of maritime traffic and maritime transport. This information is gathered by Automatic Identification System based position reports -- sent by vessels and received by coastal stations – and on notification messages (such as pre-arrival, ship's voyage and incident report notifications) sent by designated authorities in participating countries. SSN centralises this information in a single European platform. The European Maritime Safety Agency is responsible for the development, operation and maintenance of SSN, and interacts with users on an operational basis. Users of the system consist primarily of maritime administrations, port authorities, traffic monitoring services, search and rescue centres, coast guards, and pollution prevention centres.

The above examples highlight the use of GIS to prevent accidents, but it is relied on even more heavily in the direct aftermath of a disaster, particularly in its use of handheld devices. GPS-enabled devices can show up-to-date maps of vessel accidents, highlight areas of stranded wildlife or other populations at risk, and help prioritise clean-up or rescue efforts by equipping responders with critical information. Additionally, data and observations from field teams, air support, and other early responders can be incorporated into a single system that improves response strategy development and response times.

One of the unique aspects of GIS is the capacity to incorporate different mapping tools that various stakeholders already know how to use into a single, coherent picture of the information available during a crisis and how that information changes over time. This level of intelligence can greatly improve the decision-making of risk managers, policy makers, and first responders, while also improving the quality and timeliness of information delivered to populations at risk and the greater public at large.

Source: Muskat (2001; 2005) and EMSA.

---

where researchers can analyse the data. A similar strategy could be used to produce data about other complex systems. For instance, analysing social networks or news feeds could facilitate a better understanding of specific human interactions, from market crashes to spontaneous organisational structures.

Modelling complex systems

Once maps are developed that adequately describe a complex system's scope, components and various relationships, an attempt can be made to model the system. A model is anything that physically or conceptually represents something else. This report deals with conceptual models, in large part those that are based on digital tools (*e.g.* computers) that are able to process and synthesise large amounts of data and complex algorithms.

Simple systems can be modelled with relative ease. However, these systems tend to be theoretical in nature and are only loosely representative of the way in which the "real world" functions. For example, models can be used to describe an equilibrium price for any amount of supply and demand. However these two variables are not the only factors that are likely to determine the actual price of a good or service. As additional factors are included, such as taxes and tariffs, subsidies, supply controls, herd mentality, and alternative purchasing options, a model that attempts to predict an actual price becomes far more complex.

Real-world complexity adds obvious challenges to the modelling of future global shocks. When such events result within complex systems, the cascading effects are very challenging to deal with. Since these events are quite rare, models use non-empirical, often artificial data for exploratory purposes and hypothesis-testing. The difficulty lies in the large number of parameters, which must be included to model the system accurately, yet simultaneously increase the margin for error. Further, complex systems do not always act as expected, since each individual component, while easily described in isolation, may act differently when functioning in combination with different system components.

Modelling in this situation becomes much more difficult and requires more sophisticated tools. Building models of critical infrastructure systems, for instance, is challenging for several reasons, including: *(i)* data acquisition is difficult; *(ii)* each individual infrastructure is independently complicated; *(iii)* infrastructures are constantly changing and evolving; *(iv)* governing regulations are changing; and *(v)* model construction is jointly performed by government agencies, academia, and private industries (Hyeung-Sik, 2007). These challenges are not unique to modelling critical infrastructure, but are frequent in other complex systems as well.

Utility of modelling

Reliance on models to predict the precise temporal and physical features of an event is unwarranted. Most models are only able to identify the general conditions that might lead to an event, not predict one directly. Despite these limits and the challenges associated with developing robust models, it is important to develop these tools for use before, during and after disruptive events. They can also be used to show where the risks lie in normal operations as there is a drift into safety margins or stress on load capacity (Dekker, 2006). Prior to an event, models can be used to identify early warning signals by illuminating the variables that affect a systems' balance. One of the most important strengths of models is their ability to assess a number of different scenarios and slightly alter variables to determine what conditions might lead to an event with undesirable (or desirable) consequences. For instance, agent-based models have been successful in producing simulations of leverage levels in financial markets under different regulatory conditions to measure correlations with market crashes (Thurner, 2010).

During events, models can be used to prioritise the distribution of resources by providing a rational assessment of the risks to particular parts of the population, society, commerce, etc., the potential damage to each, and what resources need to be mobilised to minimise destruction or disruption (see Box 3.3). A well-defined model or tool, even if there are under-standable concerns about certain assumptions being made, can at least provide a common framework to evaluate competing needs and offer some insight as to which need deserves first consideration when it comes to scarce attention or resources. Providing a unifying framework with which to evaluate different options in assessment and response strategies offers the potential to develop solid analytical and political rationale for future decisions.

Box 3.3. **Modelling pandemics using a multi-agent interdependent security (IDS) strategy**

Effective strategies for infectious disease control rely on knowing *(1)* the dynamics of disease spread within the human population taking into account contributions by organic vectors of disease, and *(2)* how best to employ public health measures such as vaccinations, antibiotics, quarantine as well as vector control in order to stem the spread of disease and mitigate its effects. In addition, the science of such strategies must also incorporate the principles of economics, as an individual's choice to adhere to public health warnings depends upon economic indices such as cost of countermeasures, risk assessment of disease, and many other factors related to decision-making.

A team at Wharton-ISTAR is using a computational model based on multi-agent interdependent security strategy to better understand the transmission of disease. The model examines the bubonic plague epidemic of India in the late 19th century as a real-life scenario on which to assess the model and its accuracy. The model involves the creation of a network of humans (as nodes) with a scale-free distribution of human-to-human contacts. This means that a small fraction of nodes are very highly connected and new nodes preferentially attach to nodes that are already highly connected. Scale-free networks provide closer approximations of the self-organisation of real complex networks. This scale-free topology is chosen because the spread of infectious diseases is highly heterogeneous, sometimes with only certain carriers, the "superspreaders", efficiently spreading the disease through their extensive contacts with other people, while most others spread the disease more locally. The model comprises three sets of agents: the healthy individuals who are susceptible (S) to infection, the already infected individuals (I) who can transmit the disease to the healthy ones, and the individuals who are removed (R) from the infection cycle, either because they have been immunised after infection and cured, or through their demise. The work focuses on determining the actual combinations of the simulation variables (environmental risk (p), human-to-human risk (q), Δp, Δq) as well as the best method to determine these variables.

The ultimate goal is to construct a robust model with which to assess the best strategies for employing life-saving public health measures. For example, a critical factor of the success of mass vaccination programmes is individual decision-making regarding vaccination. In deciding whether to vaccinate themselves, individuals consider the cost and the risk of vaccination, the probability that they will become infected, and the risk of morbidity from such an infection. Individuals often refuse or avoid vaccinations they perceive to be risky. Demand for vaccination can also increase when individuals perceive limited vaccine supply or increasing infection risk.

Box 3.3. **Modelling pandemics using a multi-agent interdependent security (IDS) strategy** *(continued)*

Trade-offs – how to calculate them and what to recommend

Policy choices, and their associated costs and benefits, can be examined by the model:

- **Vaccination** – the incentives to vaccinate include: protection from the disease after a period of about two weeks, no longer being a source of human-to-human spread of disease and the subsequent financial and social gain from the ability to stay in the network. The cost of vaccination includes the monetary value of the vaccine as well as potential medical side-effects.

- **Antibiotic therapy** – the incentives to take antibiotics are similar to those for the vaccination intervention; however, there is no lag phase of two weeks that is required to mount an adequate immune response. The costs again are side-effects and the monetary outlay for the drugs.

- **Quarantine** – here incentives include protection from contracting the disease from another human (although there may be a risk of disease from fleas) and adverse events from drugs or vaccine. The costs are removal from the social network, with associated financial loss and social isolation.

- **Kill the rats** – (specific to plague) this incentive obviously removes the zoonotic source but may have the unintended consequence of actually increasing exposure of humans to flea-borne disease, as fleas hunt for an alternative to the rat for feed. Furthermore there is the monetary cost of instituting a rat elimination programme.

- **Combination** – a variety of combinations of these interventions could be imagined.

Source: Rubin (2010).

In addition to providing data on resource distribution, models can help determine the full extent of a crisis and the mechanisms by which the event may propagate throughout a system. As noted above, an event can have consequences that reach far across a system, and may in fact have little to do with the initial event. This information can be used to impede the spread of a crisis and limit the extent of damage. For instance, understanding the various critical infrastructure sectors that are dependent upon electricity for their operations allows planners to allocate electricity generation equipment to limit the impact of an electricity failure.

Finally, models can be used *ex post* to improve preparation for future events. Once an event has occurred and is analysed, a model can be developed using hard data and information from the actual event. Various scenarios can then be analysed to determine where changes to response plans (*e.g.* resource allocation, response times, and new technologies) could improve response to reduce the negative impacts of future events.

Foundations of good modelling

To be useful for the purposes outlined above, a model must be built on solid foundations and understand their limitations. In most cases, the availability of quality data is necessary to validate the assumptions of the model. The cultivation and curation of data in areas of importance to public policy requires significant effort and resources that are not currently put forth in many areas. The exception to this is for particularly rare or unforeseen events, for which little, if any, data is available, and where modelling can only occur by using experimental data. With few reliable data on historical events, however, there is simply less scope to calibrate the model, test assumptions, and make meaningful assessments of the present risk and what damage could result if that risk were to be realised.

Without defensible assumptions, the conclusions of the model might be accurate, unrealistic or altogether irrelevant. The assumptions of any model must be evaluated across two dimensions, their number and quality, as this could influence the model's results. For instance, long-term economic models may make assumptions, once widely held, about the economy having a recurring pull towards steady-state equilibrium. The recent financial crisis, however, has presented a strong challenge to this conventional view. Policymakers should not allow a model's results dictate decisions, but situate and interpret them within a larger view that couples experience with multiple sources of input and information.

The assumptions of each model are beset by classic dichotomy between consistency and accuracy. When estimating parameters of a model without experimental data, therefore assuming specific values for unknown drivers, a balance is sought between ensuring the model yields consistent results and allowing ever more exogenous variables to improve its precision. The assumptions that are made in building the model are also essential. When considering issues of assumption validity, it is extremely important to specify exactly what the model will be used for in order to make the relevant trade-offs with the maximum amount of transparency about any weaknesses in the model.

The second major limitation of modelling is that, despite increasingly sophisticated algorithms that describe the behaviour of humans or networks, models still rely on simplified mathematical approximations of real-life experience. This means a model or tool is only as good as the data and the identifying assumptions that underlie it. Terms such as herd behaviour, which conjure up images of animals reacting to their immediate environment like automatons, describe real phenomena that have created bubbles in technology and housing markets. Models that treat individual agents as influencing and being influenced by their environment can better approximate outcomes, but challenges remain such as integrating the consequences of changes in human consumption patterns, the effects of reputation, etc.

To ensure that models and maps of complex systems are useful for policy makers their output must be digestible from the standpoint of analysis and communication. Tools appropriate for the management of risk should lie in close proximity to the decision-making process, whereby the decision-making authority is either actively involved in the use of the model or tool or is sufficiently knowledgeable about the techniques and applications employed to assess, critique, and act on the results. Results that orient decisions toward priorities or thresholds in particular, are the most useful in making tangible connections between the science and the preparedness of response activities.

Maps and models: Understanding the connection

Mapping tools enable one to understand the structure and general features of a particular complex system. A model, on the other hand, takes into account what one knows about the organisation of the system and produces an estimate of what could happen given various inputs. Models can be developed at varying levels of specificity but are, in general, more specific than the maps which inform their development. Adequate knowledge of what the system looks like through a mapping lens that provides the basis for an abstract model that resembles the real system. To this model, one adds available data to make specific, repeatable conclusions and predictions that either lead to further analysis or can directly inform decision-making efforts.

This relationship is not one-dimensional. Although mapping tools are required to inform these mathematical modelling tools, there exists an important feedback loop from model to map, particularly with regard to physical hazards, such as natural disasters. Vulnerability models, for example, are used to estimate the extent of damage caused by a flood, earthquake, or hurricane, which can then be applied to a physical map to improve co-ordination of search and rescue efforts and communication to the public. When one thinks of mapping in mostly theoretical terms, this important feedback loop is sometimes ignored, yet it remains a crucial link in providing a visual representation of the output received from these models.

Mapping and modelling of river flooding provides a simple example of this feedback relationship. A physical map contains the essential physical components of a river (*e.g.* depth, slope, channel width, soil composition), its banks, and the resources in the area can be used as the basis for a model of flooding in the river. Water volume under various storm and seasonal conditions can be tested and the results will show where and to what extent flooding might occur. The model could also mathematically predict the likely number of hospitalisations or fatalities that result, the scale of economic damage, and the duration of the flood until water levels recede. The crucial feedback loop from modelling to mapping occurs here as this information can then be laid back over a physical map to allocate resources for building defences, plan evacuation routes, dispatch responders, and provide more detailed approximations to the public about the status of the emergency situation. The creation of mapping tools and the mathematical models they inform are an iterative process, and offer policy makers more robust, evidence-based tools to approach risk and disaster management.

Decision makers should understand the limitations of mapping and modelling, and interpret results in light of experience. The proper use of modelling in a policy context depends on the type of modelling tools that are available, their individual strengths and weaknesses, and the purpose they are used for.

Maps and models: Where are the gaps?

There have been important advances in mapping and modelling techniques as they apply to complex systems over the past several years. Nonetheless, technical improvements are needed to improve the accuracy and predictive power of modelling tools. Interface improvements are also needed to further develop the capacity to translate their results into actionable policy.

Maps of complex systems are not widely available, and when they are, they are not always compatible with other related maps that exist. The traditional notion of maps as simply geographical should be broadened in the minds of policy makers to improve understanding of complex systems. Efforts to increase the availability of maps of complex systems would be significantly enhanced by addressing the challenges mentioned above: acknowledging the complexity of the systems, the data requirements and availability, and the sustained effort needed due to the evolving nature of the systems.

Once a robust map is developed, a basis has been laid for modelling the complex system, but challenges remain. One of the most important areas that must be addressed to improve future modelling initiatives is the development of strong and defendable assumptions, particularly in areas that are far from clear cut, *e.g.* rational decision-making. Humans often have visceral reactions to events and the environment around them, and it is difficult for models to accurately depict such mutable or psychological variables. The intentions of the agents within any model are also very hard to determine and can sway results. For example, a model could be developed to analyse where a terrorist bomb attack on a subway line would cause the most casualties using data on traffic patterns (*e.g.* passengers per station per hour). Could such a model identify with high probability the stations most likely to be targeted for attack? This would certainly be very important information if the attacker's intentions were to create maximum casualties. While this might be the case, the intention could also be to carry out an attack without being caught or to strike a place of major historical or cultural significance. In this case the model's assumptions are wrong or at best incomplete, and the data associated with traffic patterns may be much less important than data about the security measures at various stations or best possible escape routes.

Another area that requires attention to improve modelling activities is the availability of data and level of appropriate surveillance. Lack of available data is a major challenge in applying mapping and modelling approaches to address pandemics. There is no source of real-time data available for pandemic risks due to a lack of infrastructure required for sufficient surveillance and reporting and a lack of initiative within the international community to fill the gaps (Rubin, 2010). Improved availability of real time data on the bacterial and viral strains present around the world, and who is being affected by them, would greatly improve modelling capacities, the identification of populations and geographical areas at risk, while informing surveillance and prevention efforts.

Where data are not available, in some cases changes to regulation could provide a legal basis for its collection. Policies for the protection of personal information and business confidentiality, however, make data collection and use by policy makers difficult. Access is resisted where the public release of data may negatively reputations or put them at risk. Organisations that have been victim of cyber-attacks might lose the confidence of customers as a result of revealing a security breach. While efforts are being made both in North America and Europe to enhance information sharing between public authorities and private sector actors, and most notably operators of critical infrastructure, a lack of confidence often persists due to insufficient safeguards. Additional research is needed to identify what conditions are needed that would encourage operators to reveal data about vulnerabilities to a very limited authorised group for purposes related to the discharge of law enforcement and national security responsibilities and the modelling of future global shocks.

Current mapping and modelling efforts generally fail to integrate the identification and treatment of emerging constructs, which are major trends or new and persistent threads of behaviour driven by a particular alignment in incentives or a technological innovation. These can ultimately have profound effects on the development and progression of complex systems. Emerging constructs often go unnoticed until they have reached a tipping point or have sufficiently impacted a vast majority of the system itself. A major challenge is simply recognising that these constructs are developing and require attention within existing models. There are two strong examples of emerging constructs in the areas of financial markets and cybersecurity.

The failings of the United States sub-prime mortgage market brought to light risky lending practices, a boom-and-bust housing market, and the reckless securitisation and bundling of poor-performing derivatives. Underlying this was a culture of grasping for short-term profit over long-term value creation, and significant structural weaknesses in the incentive structure and operations of the interdependent global economy. This emerging construct, which in many ways represented a dangerous undercurrent within the financial system, ultimately produced high-profiled bankruptcies, a wave of foreclosures, and ripple effects throughout the global economy. Its wide-ranging effects ushered in a major recession, a disastrous rise in unemployment, and a new global debate on financial regulation.

The challenge with emerging constructs is that they are rarely noticed and never mapped or understood to the level of detail necessary for appropriate public policy interventions. The actions of banks and traders within the sub-prime mortgage market were indeed so complex and poorly understood that many financial institutions and individual actors were unaware of the extent of their exposure to the risk.

Not all emerging constructs are solely, or even primarily, negative in their consequences for the complex system in which they originate. Open source technology, or the development and production process for software characterised by a distribution of the original source code to users for modification, provides a unique example. While open source has had a transformational impact on software development by allowing professionals and amateur programmers to shape, improve, customise, and protect mainstream software programs, not all results of the open source explosion are always positive. As more people have access to the underlying code that supports these software programs, there is a greater risk of piracy or other wrongdoing. Yet, this is tempered by the increased likelihood of performance-enhancing modifications and even resilience-strengthening robustness checks. Similar to the sub-prime mortgage example above, however, the arrival of open source as an accepted method of software development represents a behavioural culture shift, an undercurrent within the universe of cybersecurity and software development that will have substantial effects on the future progression of the industry and the unique risks it generates going forward.

Complex systems most often comprise components from various markets, falling within multiple regulatory regimes and overseen by various government bodies. Where policy responsibilities are rarely centred in a single office, but fall across several groups, the costs of developing cross-cutting maps and models are often difficult to allocate. Who will pay for training, development, operation and maintenance of such models? The answer depends on the situation and will at times require a creative approach to resource allocation that takes into account the multi-disciplinary and cross-sectorial nature of complex systems that can be better understood through modelling. In countries where centralised risk managers are in place, they may be best placed to undertake this task. In other countries, inter-ministerial teams may need to be developed to ensure that bureaucratic boundaries are not unintentionally superimposed upon modelling and mapping activities.

A final area that is in need of improvement is the understanding of the utility of maps and models. Modellers need to communicate to policy makers what models are and are not capable of, and policy makers need to explain to modellers their policy goals and the levers of action available to them. This two-way street is especially important in public policy areas where policy makers may not be technical experts in modelling and vice versa.

It is important that policy makers understand that while models are a powerful tool to educate policy decisions, they do not represent a quick fix. Agent-based models, for example, should not be expected to make actual predictions about financial crashes or collapses (Thurner, 2010). They can be used to clarify or identify levels of risk under given circumstances, however and potentially to illustrate relevant policy mechanisms that could be used to prevent crashes. To facilitate such essential understanding, efforts need to focus on communicating results of mapping and modelling exercises to a policy audience. This requires distilling information from modelling results into clear and actionable policy advice.

A toolkit for this project was developed as a possible first step towards achieving these goals. It provides policy makers with a brief overview of some of the mapping and modelling tools that are currently available, and an indication of how they can be used during various phases of the risk cycle.

Conclusions

- Accessibility and availability of data about complex systems often lags behind the technology to use it. The infrastructure for real time data gathering and surveillance is weak for certain important hazards, and the sophistication of maps and models has surpassed the limits of willingness to share some types of information.

- Maps and models of complex systems are rarely available, and

- There is no valid "one-size-fits-all" approach to modelling, and some models do fail to provide actionable information.

Policy options

- As a measure of redundancy, a variety of modelling approaches should be pursued to help inform risk management policy decisions.

- Mapping and modelling of future global shocks needs proper government support to ensure continuity, validation and refinement over time. In particular, models for extreme events that use experimental data in particular need to be revised as data becomes available. Information systems should be established to regularly update map dynamics and model variables. The basic assumptions in models should undergo periodic "wild-card" stress tests.

- Due to the high number of complex systems from which future global shocks could arise, there is a need to develop diverse modelling capabilities with global coverage that make use of variables derived from various disciplines, including the social sciences.

Bibliography

Apps, P. (2011), *Analysis: After the crisis, a worldwide rise in unrest?*, Thomson Reuters, London.

Asikainen, T. *et al.* (2010), "Studies needed to address public health challenges of the 2009 H1N1 influenza pandemic: insights from modeling", PLoS Medicine, Vol. 7, No. 6, PubMed, Rockville Pike.

Briesemeister, L., P. Lincoln and P. Porras (2003), Epidemic Profiles and Defense of Scale-Free Networks, SRI International, ACM, Washington, DC.

Carmi S. *et al.* (2007), A model of Internet topology using k-shell decomposition, PNAS, Vol. 104, No. 27, pp. 11 150-11 154, *www.pnas.org/content/104/27/11150.full.pdf*, last accessed 1 September 2010.

Casti, J. (2011), *Future Global Shocks: Four Faces of Tomorrow*, OECD, Paris.

CENTRA Technology (2010), Future Global Shocks Case Study: "Geomagnetic Storms", OECD, Paris.

Chai C.L. *et al.* (2008), "Social network analysis of the vulnerabilities of interdependent critical infrastructures", *International Journal of Critical Infrastructures*, Vol. 4, No. 3, pp. 256-273.

Chen, P. *et al.* (2009), "Managing Critical Infrastructure Interdependence through Economic Input-Output Methods", *Journal of Infrastructure systems*, Vol. 15, Issue 3, pp. 200-210.

Cohen, B.-A. and Havlin (2001), "Breakdown of the Internet under Intentional Attack", *Physical review letters*, Vol. 86, No. 16, 16 April.

Cohen, F. (1999), *Simulating Cyber Attacks, Defenses, and Consequences*, Fred Cohen & Associates.

Dekker, S. (2006), "Resilience Engineering: Chronicling the Emergence of Confused Consensus", in *Hollnagel.*

DIMES (2009), "The DIMES Project", *www.netdimes.org/new/?q=node/54*, accessed 27 October 2010.

ESRI (n.d.), What is GIS? *www.gis.com/content/what-gis*, accessed 27 October 2010.

Hollnagel, E., D. D. Woods, and N. Leveson (eds.) (2006), *Resilience Engineering: Concepts and Precepts*, Ashgate, Hampshire.

Hyeung-Sik *et al.* (2007), Toward modelling and simulation of critical national infrastructure interdependencies, *IIE Transactions*, 39, pp. 57-71, Thomson Gale, Farmington Hills.

Graham-Rowe, D. (2007), "Mapping the Internet", *MIT Technology Review*, 19 June, *www.technologyreview.com/infotech/18944/*, accessed 1 September 2010.

Grubesic, T. and Murray, A. (2006), Vital Nodes, Interconnected Infrastructures, and the Geographies of Network Survivability, Annals of the Association of American Geographers, 96(1), pp. 64-83, *www.cnr.berkeley.edu/~bingxu/UU/spatial/Readings/ GrubesicAnnals2006.pdf*, last accessed 10 October 2010.

Information Sciences Institute of the University of California (2009), Report on National Cyber Defense Initiative Industry Workshop, ISI, California.

Jovanovic, A., O. Renn and R. Schroter (2011), "Social Unrest", OECD Project on Future Global Shocks, OECD, Paris.

Love, J.J. (2008), "Magnetic monitoring of Earth and space", *Physics Today*, February, *http://geomag.usgs.gov/downloads/publications/pt_love0208.pdf*, accessed 4April 2011.

Muskat, J. (2001), *GIS Applications for Oil Spill Prevention and Response in California*, CA Department of Fish and Game, Proceedings of ESRI User Conference, San Diego.

Muskat, J. (2005), *GIS Imagery for Natural Resource Damage Assessment*, CA Department of Fish and Game, GIS for Oil & Gas Conference 2005, Denver, CO.

OECD (2009), Report on "Applications of Complexity Science for Public Policy: New Tools for Finding Unanticipated Consequences and Unrealized Opportunities", Global Science Forum, *www.oecd.org/dataoecd/44/41/43891980.pdf*, accessed 31 August 2010.

OECD (2011), *A strategy toolkit for Future Global Shocks*, International Futures Programme, OECD, Paris.

Pederson *et al.* (2006), "Critical Infrastructure Interdependency Modelling: A Survey of U.S. and International Research", Idaho National Laboratory, Idaho Falls. *http://cipbook. infracritical.com/book3/chapter2/ch2ref2a.pdf*, accessed 12 July 2010.

Rubin, H. (2010), *Future Global Shocks: Pandemics*, OECD, Paris.

Sommer, P. and Brown, I. (2010), *Reducing Systemic Cybersecurity Risk*, OECD, Paris.

Thurner, S. (2010), *Agent Based Models: Understanding the Leverage Cycle on National Scales*, OECD, Paris.

United States Department of Homeland Security (2007), "Economic Modelling for the Analysis of Pandemic Influenza", supplement to the National Population and Infrastructure Impacts of Pandemic Influenza Report, 15 October.

Chapter 4

Emergency management of future global shocks

Large scale disasters provide some indication of the hardship and suffering societies could encounter due to future global shocks. When many countries are simultaneously managing their own crises, however, the capacity to lend resources to neighbours is severely diminished. Effective emergency management for future global shocks entails an even higher order of co-operation than that needed to cope with national level disasters, and should be built on enhanced upstream preparation and downstream co-ordinated interventions. Policy makers need to address capacity gaps in surveillance and monitoring capabilities, readily available countermeasures and automatic back-up systems. In addition to these gaps, and in some cases at their heart, is a lack of appropriately trained human capital to manage external and internal risks that could destabilise systems and create widespread negative spillovers. This chapter considers the global capacity to conduct surveillance of potential global shocks, to activate early warning systems, and the challenge of providing incentives for the production of countermeasures and robust or diversified critical systems.

Introduction

Effective emergency management for future global shocks entails an even higher order of co-operation than that needed to cope with national level disasters. Priority setting and co-ordinated action have proven to be challenges to managing the latter, but these difficulties are greatly compounded in situations that require scaling-up resources internationally where different languages, cultural assumptions and geopolitical imperatives may impede efficiency and cohesion. The ability to manage a global shock should not begin, when possible, with efforts to control and overcome adverse impacts using rapidly assembled resources. For most known hazards there are anticipatory capabilities such as surveillance of unusual circumstances, monitoring indicators of critical thresholds and early warning systems. When dealing with unknowns, however, there are no data to drive forecasts, vulnerabilities are revealed too late to develop and deploy countermeasures and the best strategic step is to cultivate resilience.

The costs of infrastructure for surveillance and early warning systems have proven to exceed the capacity of many countries to pay. Moreover, the uncertainties surrounding extreme events make it difficult for organisations to maintain an optimal amount of emergency reserves, stockpiles, surge capacity and back-up systems to compensate for disruptions to supply or meet sudden increases in demand. Even where risks are clearly emerging, there is often a shortage of new and effective countermeasures, as well as a lack of trained personnel to handle operational aspects of emergency response. These gaps in emergency management capacity provide significant challenges to policy makers in light of the new risk landscape, which is more conducive to global shocks.

Surveillance, monitoring and early warning systems

The purpose of Early Warning Systems (EWS) is to detect sudden increases in incidence of known hazards that have the potential to cause serious socio-economic consequences and/or public health concerns. Rapid, accurate and dependable forecasts serve to inform decision makers of potential risks, but it is the ability to act on warnings that may ultimately reduce vulnerability to global shocks. Indeed, EWS take on added importance for rapid-onset events affecting complex systems, since timely interventions at key control points are the main means to prevent propagation of secondary and tertiary effects. Deepening scientific understanding of hazards and the use of modern technologies have underpinned vast improvements in EWS by linking the observance of events to timely interventions. These improvements often entail considerable capital investment and ongoing operational expenses. EWS require sophisticated sensor and communications technologies to gather and transmit vast data requirements in real time, and generally rely on highly trained experts to interpret their results and to effectively communicate their meaning to decision makers. When it comes to global shocks, the case for investing in such mechanisms is strengthened by the sheer scale of people and assets potentially exposed. Scale increases the affordability for each participant as costs can be more broadly distributed and the benefit-cost ratio increases.

Aggregate net benefits from worldwide weather forecasts are estimated to exceed costs by a factor of between 5:1 and 10:1 on average (World Bank, 2008). The ratio of benefits to costs for EWS is extremely variable, however, between specific types of hazards and depending on location – from as low as 3:1 for hurricane warnings, and 4:1 for tornado warnings, to as high as 25:1 for cyclone Sydr, 500:1 for Bangladesh floods, and 2500:1 for Philadelphia heat waves. Since early warning systems for global shocks resemble public goods, however, free–riders' effects often result in investment falling below required levels. International institutional arrangements have proven valuable to foster surveillance and information sharing for very different types of global risks. Several initiatives could be seen as models of international co-operation to provide early warning for global shocks (see Box 4.1).

The bottom-line effectiveness of EWS can be measured in terms of false positives and false negatives, and more importantly their ability to deliver useful information with sufficient lead-time so that the public acts on alerts. False positives may result when signal parameters are too broad and thresholds are set too low- thereby leading to unnecessary and expensive countermeasures, whereas false negatives can result in being caught off-guard by a foreseeable event. False negatives and positives are telling indicators of a system's failure

---

Box 4.1. **Global early warning systems**

The 26 December 2004 tsunami off the west coast of northern Sumatra caused more than 230 000 deaths. If an early warning system had been in place, many thousands of lives could have been saved by ordering populations in coastal areas to evacuate to higher ground. The tsunami was a grim reminder that early warnings can reduce risks, and drew global attention to shortcomings and gaps in early warning systems for natural disasters. Internationally, there are many examples of surveillance and early warning systems, but relatively few carry out surveillance or monitoring of risks whose direct impacts could produce a global shock. The World Meteorological Organisation's World Weather Watch system, the Food and Agriculture Organisation's rapid-onset food security alerts and the International Energy Agency (IEA) are three examples. These global institutions illustrate how the supervision of cross-border, systemically important risks requires strong international co-operation to share the burden of operational costs and clear rules, in particular regarding uncertainties that would justify erring on the side of caution.

IEA has nearly 40 years' experience in monitoring data on oil production and consumption levels in near real time to anticipate a supply-side shock, as well as a co-ordinated response system in case one should occur. The most important risks to IEA's surveillance and warning system that could undermine the accuracy of its forecasts are uncooperative reporting from producer countries and unreliable data on the demand of certain non-OECD countries.

The World Meteorological Organization (WMO) maintains networks that link national meteorological and hydrological services to support operational services 24 hours a day and seven days a week for collecting hydrometeorological and climate data. They assist in the development of thresholds and algorithms for making decisions on issuance of warnings, as well as disseminating these warnings to the public (Briceno, 2007). Moreover, the operational infrastructure of weather prediction systems within WMO's World Weather Watch system serves valuable secondary functions.

For example, the WMO's Emergency Response Activities programme tracks and predicts the spread of airborne hazardous substances in the event of an environmental emergency. The ERA programme was established in response to the Chernobyl nuclear power plant accident in 1986. The programme has focused its operational arrangements and support on nuclear facility accidents. In addition the programme has included emergency response to the dispersion of smoke from large fires, ash and other emissions from volcanic eruptions, and chemical releases from industrial accidents (WMO, 2011a).

WMO activated the ERA mechanism in the aftermath of the 11 March 2011 earthquakes and tsunami in Japan. Its centres in China, Japan and Russia are responsible in this case for predictions of the trajectories and spreading of contaminants following environmental accidents with cross-border implications. The information is made available for the use of National Meteorological and Hydrological Services to advise their respective government agencies, and for the International Atomic Energy Agency which manages nuclear safety for its State Parties.

---

or success, but they do not indicate why a problem occurred and what to do to fix it. A broader framework to assess early warning capacities contains four inter-related elements, spanning: knowledge of the risks faced, technical surveillance and warning services, dissemination of meaningful communication to those at risk, and public capacity and preparedness to act upon alerts (UNISDR, 2006). Weaknesses in any one of these elements can prevent the early warning system from serving its purpose.

The project case studies illustrate various weaknesses in the capacity of early warning systems. Overall, warning services for pandemics, cyber attacks and financial crises are clearly not as effective as for geomagnetic storms, whose precursors can usually be spotted and tracked before they threaten orbital and terrestrial assets. In some cases, *e.g.* pandemics, the underlying infrastructure to gather and analyse data is available, but in many parts of the world cost is a barrier to uptake. In the case of cyber risks, the specific hazards are not easily anticipated or observed before systems are infiltrated. Certain types of financial crisis have well-known precursors that can be monitored, such as currency crises and the bursting of asset bubbles, whereas EWS for other types of financial crisis often lack availability of or access to data.

Pandemics

Pandemics pose significant disaster risks worldwide and undermine global security and economic development. Early warning activities for pandemics are based mainly on disease surveillance, reporting and epidemiological analysis, supported by information systems that enable integration and sharing of health data. Notable improvements in regional and national capacities for early detection, confirmation and characterisation of epidemic and pandemic threats have been observed after adoption of the International Health Regulations in 2005. In most countries national surveillance systems are in place to identify and track human and animal epidemics and pest infestations, although at various stages of development and effectiveness. Institutions such as the Centres for Disease Control and Prevention in the United States and Europe provide accurate and timely information on global public health issues and are capable of quickly assessing and responding to emerging health risks around the world. In lieu of uniform surveillance infrastructures in all countries, low cost alternatives have developed to bolster situation awareness for public health threats that might otherwise fail to raise concern until it is too late to effectively use the full range of available countermeasures. Box 4.2 provides an example of the use of new technology for global surveillance of infectious disease.

Infectious disease surveillance activities in many developing countries are not considered to be capable of functioning as early warning systems. The time between case detection and reporting for most epidemics is more than the recommended 24 hours. These weak links are of global concern due to the ease with which some infectious diseases can spread quickly around the world without manifesting signs of symptoms in their hosts. The high cost of technical monitoring means infrastructure for surveillance and reporting of disease outbreaks that could become pandemics is generally not available – or is dysfunctional in many developing countries. Additional reasons for incomplete surveillance and reporting include: inadequate community-based surveillance, low index of suspicion among health workers, inadequate laboratory equipment and referral networks at local level, and weak communication and disease notification systems. Such significant differences between the capacity of industrialised countries and developing countries are likely to test any notion of global solidarity or security, with travel and trade restrictions more likely to be imposed by the former upon interactions with the latter.

Box 4.2. **Global monitoring and early warning – public health**

A notable development that boosted monitoring and early warning capacity for public health risks is the Global Public Health Intelligence Network (GPHIN). GPHIN is a secure, Internet-based "early warning" system that gathers preliminary reports of public health significance in seven languages on a real-time, 24/7 basis. This unique, multilingual system gathers and disseminates relevant information on disease outbreaks and other public health events by monitoring global media sources such as news wires and web sites. The information is filtered for relevancy by an automated process, and then analysed by the Public Health Agency of Canada, which developed GPHIN so that it could be subscribed to by anyone for a fee. Information from GPHIN is provided to the WHO, international organisations and non-governmental organisations who can then quickly react to public health incidents.

Notifications about public health events that may have serious public health consequences are immediately forwarded to subscribers. The scope of topics GPHIN tracks comprises disease outbreaks, infectious diseases, contaminated food and water, bio-terrorism and exposure to chemical and radio-nuclear agents, and natural disasters. It also monitors issues related to the safety of products, drugs and medical devices.

GPHIN provides governments, media, businesses, academia and civil society groups with the information necessary to better respond to emerging health risks around the world. The network is a low-cost, effective early warning instrument for chemical, biological, radiological and nuclear public health threats worldwide, such as emerging infectious diseases. GPHIN II is an adaptable system with multilingual capacity in Arabic, English, French, Russian, Simplified and Traditional Chinese, and Spanish. Users can review the documents in the language of their choice. It also translates articles from English to the other languages, and vice versa. In the future, additional languages will be added to GPHIN's capacity.

Source: Public Health Agency of Canada (2010).

WHO first established the Global Influenza Surveillance Network (GISN) nearly 60 years ago as the global alert mechanism for the emergence of influenza viruses with pandemic potential. The main components of the network (called National Influenza Centres – NICs) sample patients with influenza-like illness and submit representative isolates to collaborating centres (called WHO CCs) for antigenic and genetic analyses. Currently, 135 institutions from 105 countries are recognised by the WHO as NICs – the network nodes. Annually, they collect more than 175 000 patient samples and submit around 2 000 viruses to the WHO CCs – for antigenic and genetic analyses. Although there are over 800 WHO CCs in 80 countries, only six participate in the GISN. Most viruses sent to WHO CCs are sequenced to find out if they are evolving away from currently circulating strains and from vaccine strains. This effort supports the need to foresee virus characteristics that carry increased levels of risk, such as potential for human to human transmission.

Despite the relatively long history of GISN, gaps in linking disease surveillance and virological information persist. Experts claim the network nodes could collaborate better in general and better share information in particular to improve regional and global communicable disease response. To address these gaps experts claim the GISN needs to increase its geographical coverage, facilitate rapid detection of emerging variant or pandemic strains, and increase its availability of electronic communication to support real-time reporting of virological isolations and epidemiological data.

Cyber risks

Monitoring electronic information networks allows businesses, critical infrastructure operators, law enforcement and intelligence agencies to issue alerts about intrusions to end them, gather evidence to pursue hackers and to improve security procedures in light of these intrusions. Given the transnational nature of the internet, effective cybersecurity requires a co-ordinated approach to international engagement. Typically this effort revolves around:

- Investigating electronic attacks conducted for purpose of espionage, sabotage, terrorism or other forms of politically motivated violence, and attacks on defence systems;

- Collecting intelligence both domestically and internationally on such matters, assessing the capabilities and intentions of persons and groups of security interest;

- Co-operating with international agencies to investigate and prosecute technology-enabled crime and address cyber crime issues; and

- Providing a trusted environment for information exchanges between the central government and businesses on cybersecurity-related issues.

Some of these actions are typically undertaken by a Computer Emergency Response Team (CERT) and/or national CERT, where they exist. These organisations are the source of public information and a main point of contact for international cybersecurity counterparts. They are tasked with providing citizens with access to information on cyber threats and vulnerabilities so that they can better protect themselves. Capacity between CERT in different countries is highly uneven, as is the level of co-operation between different CERT, *i.e.* some CERT maintain close ties while some CERT do not speak to each other. Several international organisations (OAS, ENISA, APEC) have undertaken to establish and develop CERT capacity in a selection of countries. Box 4.3 describes a novel initiative supported by ITU that specifically aims to bolster early warning for cyberattacks and to improve the diffusion of remedial countermeasures.

Box 4.3. **Global monitoring and early warning – cyber risks**

IMPACT's Global Response Centre (GRC) operates a Network Early Warning System that was designed to help member countries identify cyber threats early on and provide critical guidance on appropriate measures to address them. The GRC is supposed to provide members of the International Telecommunications Union with access to a unique electronic tool called Electronically Secure Collaborative Application Platform for Experts (ESCAPE) that enables authorised cyber experts across different countries to pool resources and collaborate with each other remotely, yet within a secure and trusted environment. By pooling resources and expertise from many different countries at short notice, ESCAPE aims to enable individual nations and the global community to respond immediately to cyber threats, especially during crisis situations. The objective of ESCAPE is to enable the GRC to act as a "'one-stop" coordination and response centre for countries during emergencies, enabling swift identification and the sharing of available resources across borders.

Some countries have also set up separate, whole-of-government organisations to gain a comprehensive understanding of cyber threats against national interests and to co-ordinate operational responses to cyber events of national importance across government and critical infrastructure. For example, in Canada the Cyber Incident Response Centre (CCIRC) monitors the cyber threat environment around the clock and is responsible for coordinating the national response to any cyber security incident. The Centre is a key component of the government's all-hazards approach to national security and emergency preparedness. CCIRC works with national and international counterparts to collect, analyse and disseminate data on cyber threats. The Centre provides analytical releases, as well as a variety of information products and services specifically for ITC professionals and managers of critical infrastructure and other related industries.

Financial crises

The test for early warning of financial crises is arguably whether the method used provides a statistically and economically significant prediction. Since 1999, IMF has been tracking several models of currency crisis, with mixed results. It produces forecasts for currency crises with the Kaminsky (KLR) model and the Developing Countries Studies

---

Box 4.4. Global Financial Stability Map

The Global Financial Stability Map is a tool to interpret the risks and underlying conditions that impact financial stability in a graphical manner. The Map was motivated by the increased focus among policy makers on the importance of monitoring financial stability, given the increasing complexity of the underlying factors contributing to instability, the severity of the potential effects of instability on the real economy, and an apparent gap in available surveillance devices. The Map, coupled with other financial surveillance tools, seeks to create a more systematic approach to monitoring the global financial infrastructure to improve the understanding of risks and conditions that affect financial institutions and other intermediaries, and ultimately to warn policy makers and market participants about the risks of inaction.

The shifting contours of credit risk, market and liquidity risks, as well as the macro-financial conditions from the previous period reflect the IMF's view of the risks and prospects ahead. Quantitative analysis underpins the construction of this map although the final positioning is based on judgement. Leading indicators in six broad areas are considered: monetary and financial conditions in leading industrial countries, risk appetite in global financial markets, macroeconomic risks in G3 and OECD countries, emerging market risks, credit risks and market risks. When applied to past events of financial instability, IMF reports that the Global Financial Stability Map performs reasonably well in signalling risks to stability, as well as in characterising the depth of crisis episodes.

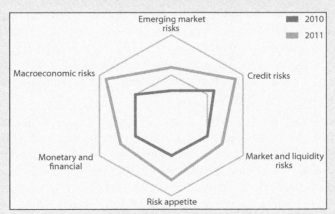

Note: Closer to centre signifies less risk, tighter monetary and financial conditions, or reduced risk appetite. This figure depicts the criteria of the GFSM published by the International Monetary Fund (April, 2011), but it is not the actual map. The purpose here is to show that global financial stability is being mapped to facilitate decisions, not to inform what the risks were on a certain date.

Division model, and it monitors two models from private sector firms- Goldman Sachs and Credit Suisse First Boston (Berg *et al.*, 2005). The KLR "leading indicator" model uses an index of exchange market pressure (EMPI) for each country, which is constructed as a weighted average of monthly percentage changes in the nominal exchange rate and in gross national reserves. These two components are weighted in such a way that they have the same conditional variance. An increase in the EMPI, either due to a currency's depreciation or due to a loss of international reserves, is considered to be a period of currency crisis if the index is more than three standard deviations above its country specific mean (Beckman *et al.*, 2006).

In addition the IMF and World Bank initiated the Financial Sector Assessment Program (FSAP) in 1999 following the Asian financial crisis. The programme aims to detect risks to a healthy financial sector in a particular country through comprehensive and in-depth financial stability assessments. The IMF deems the financial sector in 25 jurisdictions, representing almost 90% of the global financial system and 80% of global economic activity, to be systemically important based on their size and interconnectedness. For these jurisdictions, assessments are now a mandatory part of the IMF's Article IV surveillance activity, and are supposed to take place every five years. For all other jurisdictions, participation in the programme is voluntary. The 2008 financial crisis illustrated weaknesses in the programme that have since been identified and will be monitored closely in future. Among the main factors that contributed to a mixed record in the quality and usefulness of FSAPs in advanced countries were:

- Voluntary participation: some countries did not undergo an assessment despite the benefits that an in-depth examination of their financial sectors might have had;

- Outdated assessments: even when the assessments were relatively recent, they did not always identify all sources of risk: for example, liquidity risks and cross-border or cross-market linkages were under-appreciated, and where risks were accurately identified, the warnings were not always loud and clear. The Fund's Internal Evaluation Office recently recommended that mandatory assessments take place every three years for all systemically important jurisdictions (IMF, 2011).

Geomagnetic storms

Several OECD member countries have space agencies that take the lead in space weather monitoring and prediction. These organisations combine with intergovernmental initiatives and public-private partnerships to provide current capacity for space weather threat notification services. Chief among these collaborations is the International Space Environment Service (ISES), which facilitates near-real-time international monitoring and prediction of the space environment.

ISES depends on data inputs and the assets of Regional Space Weather Warning Centres (RWCs) in more than a dozen countries. A network of academic institutions, national government agencies, and regional space agencies provide the actual assets and manpower for ISES; it relies in particular on the United States NOAA National Weather Service's Space Weather Prediction Center (SWPC). In addition, the European Space Agency (ESA) plays an important role in ISES as a data exchange hub for European warning centres. Increasing numbers of government agencies and private sector entities are subscribing to the SWPC's subscription services (Bogdan, 2010).

The SWPC's role especially illustrates ISES dependence on national assets to accomplish its international mission as it provides data integration services and forecasts for the entire RWC network. Although the ESA Solar and Heliospheric Observatory spacecraft contributes important operational data to international space weather monitoring and prediction efforts (Murtagh, 2007), the system relies to a great degree on American assets. The United States NASA Advanced Composition Explorer (ACE) satellite provides real-time solar wind data that, when combined with other information, can yield real-time forecasts of geomagnetically induced currents (GIC) (Lundstedt, 2006). The Constellation Observing System for Meteorology, Ionosphere and Climate satellite programme, a joint effort between the United States and Chinese Taipei, supports the prediction of geomagnetic storms' impact on GPS satellites (Murtagh, 2007).

Although many of these satellites were launched with the explicit intention of benefiting the entire scientific community, their maintenance costs and potential replacement remain the sole responsibility of national governments. The investments that some nations have made in warning systems provide a valuable tool in helping all nations lower the risk of catastrophic consequences. While much of the international community benefits from the international geomagnetic storm-alerting system, the burden of hardware maintenance that provides space weather monitoring and prediction data falls on a few countries. The ACE satellite, in particular, illustrates this issue. The ACE satellite's orbital position allows it to provide data to support highly accurate forecast techniques and the issuance of alerts and warnings for impending major geomagnetic disturbances. Numerous space weather experts note that it is operating beyond its originally designed operational life. Yet, its replacement depends entirely on the United States as no international mechanism exists to fund a replacement (National Academy of Sciences, 2008). Today, the ACE satellite represents a critical possible point of failure in the global geomagnetic storm alert and monitoring network. The international community is relying on the United States to replace ACE. Although funds have been proposed in the 2011 budget to fund an ACE replacement, the international community should carefully consider investing in additional satellite resources to complement the ACE replacement's planned coronal mass ejection directional detection capabilities.

There is significant room for improvement to be made in the international infrastructure to issue alerts and warnings for geomagnetic storms. First, understanding the consequences of geomagnetic storms requires a greater understanding of the ground-induced currents that result. Greater investment in magnetometers worldwide and integration of the resulting data would improve capacity to assess storm severity. The international geomagnetic storm alerting and warning community currently uses a five-level scale to communicate the severity of an impending geomagnetic storm. This scale lacks sufficient granularity at the high end to provide useful tactical guidance to geomagnetic storm alerting and warning information customers. As consumers of space weather forecasting services, the electric power industry would benefit from greater granularity differentiating between severe and extreme geomagnetic storms for tailored operational mitigation measures.

Countermeasures, reserves and back-up systems

The magnitude of damages that potential global shocks could produce argues in favour of increasing the capacity to prevent, mitigate and execute extraordinary responses. In most cases where systemic risks are a possibility, regulations attempt to limit exposures, but in the case of some hazards there are no specific regulatory approaches to force firms to take precautions; although prudence and self-interest are often sufficient to prompt protective measures. Experience with natural disasters has made society familiar with such drastic measures as evacuations, quarantines, restrictions on movement and mass gatherings or even the rationing of food, water, gas, electricity and bandwidth. To avoid the need for such extreme measures, policy makers and businesses have the option to maintain adequate reserves of essential goods and to mitigate the impacts of shocks with technical solutions, but for various reasons such countermeasures are not always available or undertaken. While international co-ordination among major central banks has taken place on an *ad hoc* basis to stabilise financial markets by providing liquidity, there are relatively few examples of internationally standing mechanisms to co-ordinate reserves for the purpose of stemming a global shock.

Box 4.5. **Internationally co-ordinated energy reserves**

The International Energy Agency (IEA) emergency response mechanisms are a key example of international co-ordination to manage critical reserves in the face of a potential global shock. The Agreement on an International Energy Programme (IEP Agreement) requires IEA member countries to hold oil stocks equivalent to at least 90 days of net oil imports and – in the event of a major oil supply disruption – to release stocks, restrain demand, switch to other fuels, increase domestic production or share available oil, if necessary. Since its creation, the IEA has acted on two occasions to bring additional oil to the market through co-ordinated initiatives: in response to the 1991 Gulf War and the hurricanes in the Gulf of Mexico in 2005.

To supplement the mechanisms defined in the IEP Agreement, the IEA has elaborated flexible arrangements for co-ordinated use of stock draw, demand restraint and other measures that could be implemented in response to a disruption in oil supplies. IEA collective response actions are designed to mitigate the negative impacts of sudden oil-supply shortages by making additional oil available to the global market through a combination of emergency response measures, which include both increasing supply and reducing demand.

Although supply shortages may bring about rising prices, prices are not a trigger for a collective response action, as these can be caused by other factors and the goal of the response action is to offset an actual physical shortage, not react to price movements. Close dialogue and co-operation are maintained with consuming countries that are not member countries of the IEA and collective actions are taken in co-ordination with major producing countries.

The most significant oil-supply disruptions in recent decades have occurred in the Middle East, the largest of which was associated with the 1978 Iranian revolution. More recently, in early 2003, the market suffered disruptions from overlapping events: the effects of a strike at the national oil company in Venezuela and the outbreak of war in Iraq were exacerbated by strikes in Nigeria.

In assessing the necessity to initiate a co-ordinated action, the IEA considers multiple factors beyond the gross peak supply loss caused by the event. The decision depends on the expected duration and severity of the oil-supply disruption, and also takes into account any additional oil which may be put on the market by producer countries.

Pandemics

Among the control measures for the H1N1 pandemic were treatment with anti-viral agents for people who were ill and prophylactic treatment of all their contacts. In a pandemic situation, before a vaccine becomes available, this level of treatment and medical prevention may amount to providing anti-virals to as many as 80% of the people in an affected community. Consequently, very large supplies of the drugs must be made available; much larger supplies than could be produced on demand. Many countries have chosen to stockpile antiviral medications against pandemic influenza due to fear of global shortages and an awareness of manufacturing limitations during an outbreak. The time required to prepare and distribute an influenza vaccine means that these stockpiles are the only medical defence against widespread infection for the first six months.

One of the most significant failures in the global public health response to pandemic H1N1 was the lack of sufficient vaccine supplies in time for the second wave. Global production of influenza vaccine continues to fall well short of WHO's target of vaccine supplies, sufficient for two billion people within six months of the provision of a pandemic strain. H1N1 swine flu vaccine production amounted to only 534 million doses within the six-month milestone (WHO H1N1 Influenza Vaccine Task Force, 2010). Reasons for this shortage include lower-than-expected production yields associated with egg-based production methods (H1N1 vaccine yields were two-thirds lower than their seasonal vaccine counterparts). WHO also noted reluctance among some regulatory bodies to approve vaccines with adjuvants (immune system-enhancing additives) to stretch vaccine doses. At the same time many countries ordered far more vaccines than they actually used, in part due to the uncertainty whether one or two doses were needed for different age groups. As the pandemic continued its course, demand declined and production capacity was set aside for seasonal flu vaccine.

Governments facing important budget pressures need to improve the accuracy of demand-forecasting for vaccines leading up to a pandemic, and especially in its initial phase. Several OECD countries ended up discarding millions of expired doses of H1N1 vaccine in 2010, after many developing countries could not access the vaccines. If the virus characteristics are thought to be so dangerous that they require ordering enough vaccine for the entire population, government contracts with producers should negotiate in advance the possibility to cancel orders if the virus turns out to be less lethal than anticipated. The global response to H1N1 underscored a lack of internationally coordinated plans to send vaccines where and when they may have the greatest global health impact, and the need to augment global vaccine production capacity.

As recently as 2006, influenza vaccine production was centred in nine industrialised countries, but as seen in Figure 4.1 some vaccine production capacity is now expanding. Among the measures to bolster pandemic vaccine production in the short term, governments could consider shifting vaccine production from egg-based methods to cell-cultures, improved seed strains and testing as well as larger and more modernised facilities. Among the longer-term public policies towards the same goal would be support for adjuvenated vaccines, improved capacity to test and develop vaccines against pandemic virus threats, research towards a universal vaccine, and improved guidance from regulatory bodies to streamline approvals.

The effectiveness of non-pharmaceutical interventions to stop or slow the spread of infectious disease tends to be time-sensitive. Policy makers may put in place restrictions with a broad range of invasiveness/constraint and eventual drag-on economic activity. Among the measures available are closing border crossings and international trade; human and animal quarantines; school closures and prohibitions of large meetings. Identifying the most effective and efficient policy mix to slow the spread of infectious disease remains a race against time for each outbreak due to knowledge gaps in epidemiological dynamics of spread; the availability and cost of personal protective equipment; compliance among healthcare workers in the use of personal protective equipment and hygiene measures; and immune status of healthcare workers.

Figure 4.1. **Worldwide influenza vaccine production**

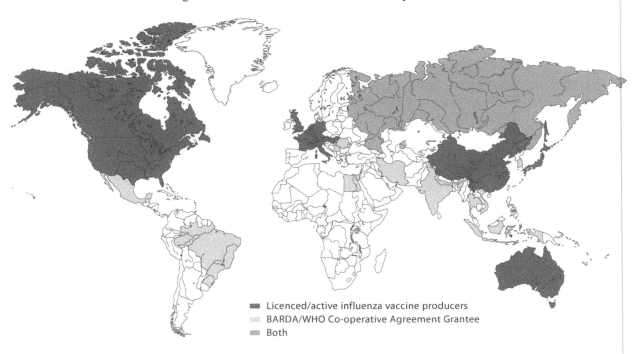

■ Licenced/active influenza vaccine producers
▨ BARDA/WHO Co-operative Agreement Grantee
▩ Both

Source: Globalhealth.gov (2010), available at *www.globalhealth.gov/images/01112010vaccinemap.jpg*, January.

Box 4.6. **Swine flu in 1976: An example of overreaction**

In the winter of 1976, a small number of soldiers at Fort Dix in the United States were infected by a strain of the flu that had not been seen in humans before. Only one of them died, but the incident caught the eye of health officials and triggered a national response, one largely criticised after the fact as a massive overreaction. Epidemiologists found that some of the sick soldiers – and the deceased one – were infected with a strain of influenza found in pigs. Fearing that a new strain of flu was about to sweep through the population like the 1918 Spanish flu pandemic – and that it might even be the same strain as that infamous disease – calls were made for a national immunisation campaign. Despite mounting evidence that the swine flu was not a serious threat, preparations for a massive vaccination programme were undertaken. Soon after the programme began, though, critics of the effort emerged, and so did evidence that the "swine flu" did not pose the threat of a pandemic at all. Nonetheless, more than 40 million people were vaccinated against it.

Some vaccinations carry a risk of adverse side-effects. Although a very low percentage of recipients experience adverse effects, the severity may range from temporary illness to serious disability. The vaccine for 1976 swine flu is believed to be responsible for hundreds of people developing Guillain-Barre Syndrome, a rare neurological disease characterised by loss of reflexes and temporary paralysis. Hundreds of lawsuits were filed against vaccine producers, resulting in about USD 100 million in settlements and judgments. Similar episodes have taken place in many OECD countries leading to the same important lesson for decision makers: acknowledge the side-effects and treat the victims well, otherwise the public's trust will be undermined and future efforts at mass vaccination will suffer lower rates of compliance.

The WHO schema for declaring influenza pandemics has come under criticism for its exclusion of severity from the operative criteria, despite the fact that there is no reliable way yet to predict it in advance. From Phase 4 onwards, political pressure tends to mount in support of expensive prevention and protection actions, for example: school closures, support for vaccination development and the use of anti-viral stockpiles. While several governments were severely criticised for overreacting to the H1N1 pandemic, no government wishes to be accused of negligence due to inaction. In fact, many governments placed massive orders for vaccines well before WHO declared the H1N1 pandemic. On the other hand, the opportunity costs associated with control measures such as social distancing and massive prophylaxis may be quite high if the pandemic turns out to not be severe. These costs include lost and misdirected productivity, and diluted effectiveness of countermeasures against future outbreaks. Timing the issuance of control measures is the key; if governments implement them too late they may be ineffective in limiting the spread of the disease, but if they put them in place too early the resulting high-opportunity costs may turn out to be difficult to justify.

Cyber risks

A number of countermeasure tools and preventive techniques are widely available in the field of cybersecurity. In fact, the security of information and communications networks has been one of the fastest growing ICT sectors over the past 15 years. While certain countermeasures to protect systems entail the purchase of expensive back-up systems or goods, other countermeasures involve the institution of policies. For global shocks, no single countermeasure is likely to suffice, but rather a wide range of countermeasures must be employed in a co-ordinated information-security strategy.

This growth is directly tied to an increase in various forms of cyber crimes, such as industrial espionage and commercial fraud. Software and hardware developers have been largely remiss in applying effective security standards to their products, leaving it to end-users to purchase anti-virus software and other complement goods at an additional cost, or run the risk of exposure to malware. The many prevention tools and countermeasures available include: user patches, encryption, file back-ups, access controls, honeypots, user education and police investigation. Nevertheless, cyber espionage and sabotage reach new levels every year. The lack of powerful general countermeasures means that attacks on computer systems and networks will continue to increase in the future. A shift in the character of cyber attackers, from amateurs to professionals, emerged at least ten years ago and will continue as basic countermeasures become more effective at deterring amateurs. The future of effective countermeasures relies on improvements in hacking forensics, back-tracing and deception. Despite their weaknesses, countermeasures do help protect systems to the extent that they have raised the necessary level of sophistication required by an attacker to succeed.

Among the possible, although unlikely, global shock scenarios due to cyber attacks are large-scale data losses, prolonged disruptions to the Internet, and destruction or malfunction of telecommunications infrastructure that are heavily relied upon for connectivity to it. As data storage becomes cheaper per unit, it will become increasingly efficient for organisations (both public and private) to diversify back-up systems at various off-site locations, which addresses the first scenario. The principal techniques to limit impacts of the second and third scenarios are alternative web routing, and distributed back-up power transmission.

Governments play a key role in co-ordinating responses to large-scale emergencies, and are as dependent as businesses on communications infrastructures to do so. The European Network and Information Security Agency (ENISA) undertook a cross-EU exercise during 2010 to ensure European Union member states are able to cope with a simulated loss of connectivity while still providing key services (European Commission, 2009). The United States Department of Homeland Security sponsors the "Cyber Storm" exercises every two years, which simulate large-scale cyber attacks on the United States government and the nation's critical infrastructure to test the response of government and industry cybersecurity personnel. In addition to 12 other countries, multiple industries participated in Cyber Storm III, including: banking and finance, chemical, communications, dams, defence, information technology, nuclear, transport, and water supply.

Financial crises

The emergency response to the 2008 global financial crisis was managed in great part by various fiscal stimulus packages to restore stability and stimulate lending, initially to firms and later to sovereign States. The United States executed two stimulus packages, totalling nearly USD 1 trillion during 2008 and 2009. Central banks around the world expanded money supplies to avoid the risk of a deflationary spiral, in which lower wages and higher unemployment lead to a self-reinforcing decline in global consumption. There has never been a globally co-ordinated response of such scale to this type of event, thus no evidence is available to support predictions on the long-term effects. The concern of moral hazard, well-understood in other sectors, is at the centre of debate. Will the recapitalisation of illiquid firms and states create the anticipation of future bail-outs, and encourage irresponsible behaviour by even more actors? Future research must be attuned to this question in order to discern the conditions under which it is a valuable tool for the next crisis.

The United States Federal Reserve, the European Central Bank, the Bank of Japan and several others purchased co-ordinated to purchase USD 2.5 trillion of government debt and troubled private assets from banks. This was the largest liquidity injection into the credit market, and the largest monetary policy action, in world history. Governments in Europe and the United States also raised the capital of their national banking systems by USD 1.5 trillion, by purchasing newly issued preferred stock in their major banks. By creating money and inserting this directly into banks the intent was to spur more domestic loans and refinance mortgages. Among the mechanisms used in OECD countries to re-stabilise markets were the 'Troubled Asset Relief Program' (TARP) and the European Financial Stability Facility (EFSF). TARP is a United States government programme originally intended to purchase assets and equity from financial institutions to strengthen the financial sector, but was subsequently revised to allow purchase of both "troubled assets, and any other asset the purchase of which the Treasury determines is necessary to further economic stability" (Congressional Budget Office, 2009). In practice this has meant that in addition to financial institutions, two automakers have received TARP funds. As part of the EUR 750 billion crisis mechanism to safeguard financial stability in Europe, EFSF was created in June 2010. Its mandate is to raise funds in capital markets in order to finance loans for peripheral euro area member states, which have been experiencing difficulty in obtaining financing at sustainable rates. The EFSF can issue bonds or other debt instruments on the market with the support of the German Debt Management Office to raise the funds needed to provide loans to euro area countries in financial trouble, recapitalise banks or buy sovereign debt.

The sheer size of these emergency mechanisms dwarfs any disaster response in the past, and the magnitude of funds directed at beneficiaries raises legitimate concerns of waste and corruption. When governments have provided relief funds to individual victims of natural disasters, the underlying rationale has usually been that public solidarity justifies such expenses when people are made destitute due to no fault of their own. TARP and EFSF are rescue packages for organisations that willingly engaged in risks and managed them poorly. The justification, therefore, is not public solidarity, but rather the need to stem systemic risk that could have resulted in a long and deep recession with innocent third parties suffering massive unemployment due to the actions of relatively few risk takers.

The next step in the response to the financial crisis has aimed directly at preventing banks from engaging in similar behaviour in future. The depth and severity of the crisis were amplified by weaknesses in the banking sector such as excessive leverage, inadequate and low-quality capital, and insufficient liquidity buffers. It also showed that some financial institutions were so interconnected with other financial companies that they posed a risk to the entire financial system. At national level, some countries have taken aim at reducing the size of banks to preclude any "too big to fail" institutions. The crisis was exacerbated by the interconnectedness of systemically important financial institutions; hence the international response has seen the Basel Committee on Banking Supervision develop a reform programme to improve the banking sector's ability to absorb shocks arising from financial and economic stress, whatever the source, thus reducing the risk of spillover from the financial sector to the real economy. As described in Box 4.7, the reforms aim to strengthen bank-level regulation, which will help raise the resilience of individual banking institutions in periods of stress. The reforms also have a macro prudential focus, addressing system-wide risks, which can build up across the banking sector, as well as the pro-cyclical amplification of these risks over time. The micro and macro prudential approaches to supervision are interrelated, as greater resilience at the individual bank level reduces the risk of system-wide shocks. Caution is warranted, however, before applying these same capital requirements to all financial institutions based only on their size as determined by capital assets and market share. An argument can be made that supervisory focus should rather be on risk activities and not institutions. As discussed in Chapter 2, system diversification can be an important feature of resilience to shocks. Applying a "one size fits all approach" to global financial regulation might have undesirable consequences, such as reducing the risk capacity of the (re)insurance industry, which would undermine its role as risk-absorber and provider of long-term financing to the real economy at times it is most needed (Karl and Frey, 2010).

Beyond the international overhaul of the framework for financial regulation, recent flash-crashes in financial markets have led to a closer look at the use of circuit breakers. A 20-minute rout on 6 May 2010 erased USD 862 billion from the value of United States equities before prices rebounded. The flash crash was the biggest points fall in the history of the Dow Jones blue-chip index. It is thought to have been caused by a chain of events unwittingly triggered by a mutual fund company that traded in a series of futures contracts. An ensuing drop in Wall Street stocks accelerated when the NYSE's circuit breaker mechanism kicked in, halting computer-driven trades and forcing brokers to execute transactions manually. This had the unforeseen effect of pushing rapid computer driven trades onto less liquid markets. Regulators believe that discrepancies between "circuit breakers" on different exchanges fuelled this unprecedented volatility (Johnsen and DiFiore, 2010).

The circuit-breaker rule says that trading in a security stops for five minutes if that security's price moves 10% or more within five minutes. Securities regulators in the United States initially expanded the number of stocks that would trigger circuit breakers to maintain market confidence in face of extreme volatility triggered by erroneous trades. Concern that halting stock trades to limit price volatility does more harm than good, however, has led to proposals to modify the program. The new plan would prevent prices from moving beyond specified bands based on a security's average level during the previous five minutes. The new rule would also allow securities to stop trading. If a stock price rises or falls to the threshold and trades are "unable to occur within the price band for more than 15 seconds," a five minute pause would be imposed to give investors time to respond to fundamental price moves driven by news about companies. Critics, however, consider market volatility to be a by-product of the dynamism of capital markets that reflects periods of strongly differing views on valuation (Serritella, 2010).

Box 4.7. **International regulatory reform: financial markets post crisis**

Collectively, the new global standards to address both firm-specific and broader, systemic risks have been referred to as "Basel III", and comprised the following building blocks to be phased in over time:

Raising the quality of capital to ensure banks are better able to absorb losses; increasing the risk coverage of the capital framework; raising the level of the minimum capital requirements; introducing an internationally harmonised leverage ratio to contain the build-up of excessive leverage in the system; raising standards for the supervisory review process and public disclosures, together with additional guidance in the areas of sound valuation practices, stress testing, liquidity risk management, corporate governance and compensation; introducing minimum global liquidity standards consisting of both a short-term liquidity coverage ratio (LCR) and a longer-term, structural net stable funding (NSF) ratio; and promoting the build-up of capital buffers in good times that can be drawn down in periods of stress, including both a capital conservation buffer and a countercyclical buffer to protect the banking sector from periods of excess credit growth.

Importantly, a comprehensive assessment of Basel III's potential effects, both on the banking sector and on the broader economy, has been undertaken. This work concludes that the transition to stronger capital and liquidity standards is expected to have a modest impact on economic growth. Moreover, the long-term economic benefits substantially outweigh the costs associated with the higher standards.

Geomagnetic storms

Evidence that predates modern infrastructure indicates that there is a risk of extremely severe geomagnetic storms with potential to cause damage on a continental or global scale. The consequences of such an event would require international co-operation for response and restoration of multiple critical infrastructure sectors. As described earlier in the chapter, monitoring of space weather is fairly advanced. Coronal mass ejections, for example, are monitored as they occur so that there is 2-3 lead time before they produce effects by interacting with the earth's magnetosphere. Even with warning and alert procedures in place, operational mitigations may be overwhelmed by a sufficiently large storm. Hardening all critical infrastructures against geomagnetic storms is neither economically cost-effective nor technically possible. Industries have been left largely to regulate their own approach to mitigating the effects of geomagnetic storms on their activities.

Satellite operators do not possess a wide range of options to prevent or mitigate geomagnetic storm risk. Satellites in Geostationary Earth Orbit (GEO) can be temporarily moved into a graveyard orbit, an orbit hundreds of miles above a satellite's normal geosynchronous orbit, where spacecraft are placed at the end of their operational life. However, this requires significant fuel, and moving large numbers of GEO satellites into graveyard orbit in a short period of time preceding an extreme geomagnetic storm would require significant co-ordination between commercial satellite operators and national governments. Hardening a satellite's electronics serves as the primary space weather risk mitigation option. But, by increasing the satellite's weight, hardening makes it more expensive to launch. So, hardening is not frequently used in commercial satellite construction. Even if a satellite is hardened, geomagnetic storms can interrupt satellite communication with ground stations, making command and control difficult and interrupting the flow of information from the satellite (NOAA, n.d.).

As for terrestrial assets, one possibility is to harden high-voltage transmission lines with transmission line series capacitors and the transformers connected to these lines through the installation of neutral-blocking capacitors. To do so for all utilities supporting 345 MV and above would prove economically exorbitant (Molinski, 2000). Since the 1989 Quebec electricity outage, for example, Hydro-Quebec has spent more than USD1.2 billion on transmission-line series capacitors (Government of Canada, 2002). Although hardening all high-voltage transmission lines and transformers is not likely to be an economically viable strategy, electricity generation companies and publicly owned utilities could harden transformers connecting critical electricity generation facilities to their respective electrical grids. Ensuring the survival of these high-voltage transformers in the event of an extreme geomagnetic storm scenario would facilitate faster restoration of national electrical grids and remove part of the likely demand for replacement high-voltage transformers.

The United States National Aeronautics and Space Administration (NASA) has created a new project called "Solar Shield" in an effort to prevent damage to key transformers in the case of a severe geomagnetic storm. Solar Shield has the potential to shelter high-voltage power lines that crisscross over North America by forecasting conditions and attempting to predict what specific transformers will be hit the hardest by geomagnetically induced currents. Since a coronal mass ejection typically takes 24 to 48 hours to cross the sun-earth divide the Goddard Community Coordinated Modelling Center (CCMC) has time to gather physics-based computer programs to model it. Thirty minutes before impact, the ACE spacecraft uses its sensors to make in situ measurements of the CME's magnetic field, density and speed, then sends the data to the Solar Shield team on Earth. The data is fed into CCMC computers where models predict currents and fields in Earth's upper atmosphere and transmit this information to the ground. The Solar Shield team is then prepared to send alerts to utilities with details about the GICs. With more power companies joined to the research effort, more data could be collected from the field to test and improve Solar Shield. While Solar Shield has never been tested during a geomagnetic storm, a small number of utilities have already installed monitors at main locations in the power grid so that the CCMC team can check their predictions (Phillips, 2010).

Incentive structures contributing to systemic risks

The incentives structures in a number of critical industries have resulted in the creation of significant externalities with destabilising effects in many systems vital to the functioning of modern society. Over the past ten years, hacking and malware have flourished, while at the same time vendors deliver a multitude of patches to remedy vulnerabilities in software products already on the market. This is a sign that information security failure results in part from perverse incentives to rush products to market before they have been adequately tested (Andersen and Moore, 2008).

A lack of proper incentives can be equally obstructive to the development of effective countermeasures. For example, investment is anaemic in the discovery and development of new antimicrobials and vaccines due to the inability to recoup sufficient profits in the face of high development costs. If this trend continues, public health at a global level will suffer as resistance grows in highly infectious and dangerous bacteria to the current stock of antibiotics. In the presence of such market failures there is a role for public policy to create the conditions under which industry has the proper incentives to provide solutions.

Providing end-users with full protection from risks is not advantageous to the producers of goods and services in terms of the optimal level of investment. At some point, the costs of adding more layers of protection exceed the benefits from carrying on the activity. As a result, firms need to determine whether they can produce an acceptable level of risk and price additions over and above it accordingly. Individual actors make their own decisions about what level of risk is acceptable, but from the perspective of the vulnerability of society, there might be additional costs to everyone that no one factors into their individual decisions. In other words, the optimal level of protection from potential risks may not be reached due to prevailing incentive patterns among consumers. This phenomenon is well-known in the domain of industrial activity that produces pollutants with risks to human health. It also applies to the development of antibiotics and new drugs to combat infectious diseases, in the realm of cybersecurity via the protection of the world's hardware and software frontiers, and to financial markets when exorbitant levels of leverage are used. In these cases too, the current pattern of incentives is leading to increased vulnerability to future global shocks.

Pandemics

The need to create new, more effective antibiotics has been significantly slowed by a lack of investment, due in part to the low success rate and lengthy time horizon that characterises the development process, a lower expected pay-off from antibiotics when compared to agents aimed at more chronic ailments, and consolidation in the pharmaceutical industry. Though the focus here is on antimicrobial development, similar incentive issues can also be applied to vaccine development, and the larger class of neglected disease drug therapies as a whole. This represents a serious problem for three interrelated reasons:

- First, new antibiotics are desperately needed to keep pace with the development of new bacteria that have developed resistance to approved treatments. New pathogens, both environmental and human-designed, or epidemics, represent constant threats which need to be matched with the drug development capable of reducing the overall threat level.

- Second, resistance to antibiotics represents a serious danger to society at large. Overuse of antibiotics and the natural evolution of certain microbes have resulted in greater resistance to some of the drugs the public health community continues to rely on heavily. One of the chief sources of this resistance is the overuse of these antibiotics in animal feed as a growth enhancer. As a result, some human patients go untreated, while others must be subjected to greater levels of toxicity or less-than-ideal mixes of drugs to see improvement in their condition.

- Finally, research into antibiotic and advanced drug development has a number of positive externalities to the medical and public health professions, as well as other industries and society overall. Greater funding and investment for advanced scientific research, specifically in the areas of treatment for disease and drug development produces direct beneficial results for the medical community, but also results in greater collaboration on technologically advanced projects with a potentially high financial and non-financial return.

The emergence of antibiotic-resistant micro-organisms is thought to be due in part to treating human patients, but also due to overuse in agriculture. In both cases, there is often a short-term perspective to "use them while they work", which mortgages the future of public health to address current vulnerabilities. Simply prohibiting the use of antibiotic classes important to human health in animal feed might slow the trend of antibiotic resistance, but it does nothing to create incentives for developing new anti-bacterial products. The two major disincentives for pharmaceutical companies to invest in new antibiotic development are direct costs (research and development, regulatory approval process, marketing) and the opportunity cost of short-use broad spectrum drugs, forgoing the more lucrative markets in narrow, long-term use drugs (*e.g.* those used for diabetes, heart disease and cholesterol control).

Incentivising a renewed interest in the development of antibiotics is a critical public policy challenge for many countries. The United States and the European Union, in particular, have both taken steps to call attention to the issue and explore creative policy options. A number of initiatives are worth consideration in changing incentive structures to facilitate greater investment in antibiotics. Currently, antibiotic drug development remains an incredibly costly enterprise in terms of financial outlay and time, requiring investments that are only available via the largest firms. Increasing the amount of collaboration and cost-sharing among private enterprise, academic institutions, and government entities could improve the science as well as help to better allocate the R&D costs among multiple actors. Providing incentives for a greater number and more extensive public-private partnerships could encourage more focused attention on development to combat antibiotic-resistant pathogens. Other measures, including greater standardisation, tax incentives, and fast-tracking patent applications could significantly lower the barrier to entry.

Measures are needed that go beyond simply reducing the costs of development. To increase firm benefits, patent protection extensions could increase the expected pay-out period of a marketable antibiotic. In addition, there is scope to sponsor prize competitions (*e.g.* an X-prize) and for governments to enter into advance purchase contracts. X-prize competitions provide a sufficiently large pay-out and support to any company or organisation in pursuit of a particular product or goal. This has been advanced as a potential tool in the development of cancer drugs, space exploration, fuel efficiency, and the reduction of the time and costs associated with genome sequencing. Such innovative approaches could foster more intense competition, allow the entry of smaller players and firms, and generate a heightened interest from researchers and policy makers alike on a topic of critical importance.

Cyber risks

The security of information and communication technology also suffers from a sub-optimal incentive structure, particularly when it comes to guiding investments towards increasing the safety and resilience of hardware and software components for the general public. The ubiquity of anti-virus products, firewalls, and other protection products on the market is just a small indication of the depth of the concern over the potential vulnerabilities of trafficking information on the Internet. Although studies have shown that the Internet's architecture is fairly robust in the abstract and unlikely to be irreparably damaged by a single attack, private consumers worldwide are, knowingly and unknowingly, subjected to millions of spyware, malware, and virus intrusions every day, and these attacks are expected to grow.

For the cybersecurity marketplace this holds significance as recent research suggests that consumers and businesses are willing to take some risk in order to capitalise on the convenience of online transactions. The Internet Confidence Index, released by RSA security, showed that the growth in online transactions was surpassing that of confidence in the system's overall security. At the time of the release of the first index, security was failing to keep pace with what end-users wished to do online. As a result, the question of how the current level of security is determined in the marketplace and exactly who can be expected to make investments in security to account for any shortfall is a matter of personal security and is driven by the current incentive structure.

Vendors of software and hardware products and Internet Service Providers (ISPs) are in better positions to improve important aspects of cybersecurity, but it is the end-users, not the companies that create and distribute the ICT products, who bear the brunt of costs from malware and security breaches. Most producers of ICT do not have an incentive to make large-scale investments to improve security of their products as the cost generally outweighs the benefits, which include avoiding potential liabilities. Likewise ISPs do not have incentives to root out malware from their networks despite being in the best position to detect infected machines. ISPs monitor systems for abnormally high e-mail activity, which is most likely to be spam from a botnet, but there is no monetary incentive to notify individual users and help disinfect machines. There is some evidence that some ISPs' quarantine-infected machines, blacklist abusive IP addresses, contact customers, manage abuse notifications and block the most commonly used ports by malware (Asghari, 2010). Nevertheless, even the most pro-active ISPs only mitigate a fraction of externalities caused by their customers. A very small percent of the infected machines show up in abuse notifications and blacklists, and even fewer are quarantined.

It could be argued that firms are making optimal investment decisions based on their particular cost-benefit analyses, since the true costs of breaches are borne by the end-user. Producers will only have monetary incentives to increase their investments in the security infrastructure, if the network is so infected that certain ISPs become useless or consumers become so frustrated with a particularly porous software product that demand shifts to a competitor or evaporates. How to create proper incentives to reduce systemic ICT risk needs to take account of three main issues:

- Producers do not bear the full brunt of the cost of security vulnerabilities in their marketed products and make suboptimal investments in protecting their products from society's point of view;

- The networked nature of the Internet and other computer systems ensures that the level of security in one computer affects the overall level of security faced by all computers and users within the network;

- The dense web of laws, regulations, and popular perceptions regarding the prevalence of cybersecurity threats creates both a moral hazard problem (*e.g.* end-users may think they are immune or covered in the event of an attack) and information asymmetries (*e.g.* end-users are unaware of the extent of their vulnerability).

Two recent trends signal hope for improved network security without directly regulating vendors and ISPs. First, the rise of open-source technology has the potential to make systems increasingly robust to widespread attacks. Open source provides for greater collaboration, more timely adjustments, and capitalises on the accumulated knowledge of millions of participants, not just the original manufacturer of the system to improve its quality, robustness, and resilience. Second, the rise of mathematics-based security and the use of white-hat hackers, who are professional hacking experts employed to locate and patch potential vulnerabilities. ICT security divisions are even taking advantage of the diffusion of computer expertise in designing innovative competitions and games to address cybersecurity issues. In March 2009, 3Com sponsored a competition in Canada for white-hat hackers to break into five of the most popular "smart phones" to identify key security vulnerabilities.

Yet, there is still the question of whether there are additional avenues in which public policy could intervene to improve both the current incentive structure as well as the resultant set of security outcomes. To incentivise greater investment in security, the threat of bearing the costs of an attack must be allocated appropriately. Some have suggested the following questions point to possible policy avenues: Should product liability laws hold ICT producers accountable for porous products? To what extent can end-users be held responsible for their machine's use in a zombie attack (*i.e.* hold end-users accountable for negligent protection of their computer, which is then used by a remote third-party to attack a different computer)? What other avenues exist for the government to protect critical national infrastructure? These are just a few of the major questions that need to be addressed as part of a comprehensive review of the incentive structures and their appropriate policy antidotes.

Both in the realm of public health and cybersecurity, prevailing incentive structures contribute to a lack of investment in countermeasures that could reduce societal vulnerabilities. Assessing the current incentive structures and the market forces at play is required to understand potential avenues for effective policy to improve the equilibrium outcome. The answer is neither simply an increase in government regulation, nor is it entirely in the purview of the private sector. For any marketplace in which there exist significant externalities, public and private actors will need to work together to produce socially optimal levels of investment in both arenas.

Insufficient skills and knowledge to manage global shocks

Pandemics

Surge capacity in the healthcare system refers to its ability to manage a sudden or rapidly progressive influx of patients within the currently available resources at a given point in time. The 2008-09 H1N1 pandemic confirmed surge capacity as one of the most important responses to mitigate the impact of a pandemic on a country's healthcare system. In several countries the H1N1 pandemic revealed a lack of diagnostic lab capacity, healthcare facilities and personnel, which heightened the number of severe illnesses. Although the majority of people infected by H1N1 had self-limiting infections, some developed very severe forms of illness. Preliminary data indicated that approximately 20% of hospitalised cases required care in an intensive care unit. In order to prevent such severe cases, early treatment was crucial, and it has been suggested that late treatment in the country where H1N1 was first identified was associated with a higher fatality rate.

The medical sector would be critically impaired in the event of a severe pandemic, with the obvious and profound knock-on effects for the rest of society. Even if all the financial resources were available to carry out preparation plans, absenteeism and uncertainty in the supply chain could cripple the healthcare sector in the event of a severe pandemic [Ruben, 2010]. Several public policies have been known to undermine surge capacity. Mandatory vaccination of all healthcare professionals in case of pandemic influenza might reduce the spread of an outbreak, but it has resulted in threats of refusal to report to work, which would significantly reduce surge capacity. Where general practitioners can be held liable for misdiagnosis of novel influenza and liability insurance does not provide indemnity, physicians in some countries have threatened to refuse patients. Ironically, healthcare facilities that are unable to provide sufficient surge capacity may be held liable for medical malpractice if patients suffer as a result.

Financial crises

One explanation offered for the excessively high risks undertaken before the 2008 financial crisis is that a tragic misperception of risk led to inaccurate assessments produced by models. If the management of some major financial firms lacked understanding of the risks they faced, it is also accurate to say market regulators did not intervene to save them from themselves. A major lesson for financial institutions to draw from the financial crisis is to strengthen their risk management departments with better training, and ensure internal oversight at the level of the Board with good risk management principles. Box 4.8 lists a number of indicators that suggest there might be a lack of risk oversight capacity on a Board.

The governing bodies of pension funds have been extensively studied to determine whether trustees may lack the understanding to judge advice they receive from experts. This problem of board competency results directly from the often-deficient methods through which trustees are elected/selected for pension boards (Clark, 2007). The board competency issue raises questions over the contribution of member representatives to decision-making on complex matters relating to the pension fund orientation. For example, member representatives may not have the necessary knowledge and understanding of investment matters and may not feel comfortable challenging investment advisors or the plan sponsor's senior executives sitting on the board.

Box 4.8. **Indicators of potentially weak board oversight in banks**

1. Defining the risk appetite of the bank is not a top board priority; oversight of risk management and setting of risk appetite is not a core board responsibility.

2. There is no distinct risk committee, it holds a low number of yearly meetings, or is unresponsiveness to imminent risks.

3. Large variance between chief executive and senior executive pay reflects a misalignment of incentives. Similarly a lack of alignment between long-term shareholder value and CEO/Chairman's personal wealth indicates a concentration of executive power within the bank and its team culture.

4. Long tenure of CEOs/Chairmen and of non-executive directors on the board may indicate a lack of independence and in some cases competence. Inadequate/ relevant expertise on the Board undermines oversight, which underlines the importance of financial industry expertise.

5. Ageing Board, or a lack of age limits on board members indicates a highly influential CEO/Chairman with unbalanced power, no "independence of mind", lack of informational flow of regular business into board, low variation on perspectives, and potentially outdated approach to a highly dynamic and complex business.

Source: ACCA (2008).

Cyber risks

Success in combating cyber attacks involves building a highly trained and dedicated cybersecurity workforce, the quality and quantity of which is insufficient in most countries. Currently, a shortage of trained experts and fragmented governance hinder the ability to meet some key government cybersecurity workforce needs. Necessary vetting procedures complicate recruiting and retention efforts. Looking ahead, the pipeline of potential new talent is inadequate in OECD countries. As delivery of government-sponsored benefits and interactions with the general public (*e.g.* electronic voting) increasingly pass to online platforms, the scope of cybersecurity issues facing the public sector will take on even greater importance.

In the United States, a survey of 700 information security professionals working within government agencies or for government contractors revealed the frequent perception of a gap between the current information security certification programmes and specific cybersecurity skills needed in government (CSIC, 2010). While close to a majority of respondents agreed this gap exists, 69% of respondents opposed a proposal to establish a Board of Information Security Examiners to enforce certification requirements designed to close the skills gap. The licensing system for information security professionals proposed would be similar to the one for Certified Public Accountants and medical professionals. A full 48.7% of survey respondents opposed imposing a licensing system on information security professionals, more than double the number who supported the proposal. Instead, most respondents favoured working within the current system to improve the quality of information security certifications.

Conclusions

Effective emergency management of global shocks requires the availability of adequate countermeasures (*e.g.* medical, technological and financial solutions); the mobilisation of significant reserve and surge capacity (*e.g.* energy, food, water and first responders); rapid delivery of countermeasures and reserves for maximum effect; and broad deployment across multiple jurisdictions.

These factors face significant capacity gaps and risk-governance deficiencies.

1. Stockpiles, reserve capacity and other back-up solutions are generally costly to maintain, and there is a clear pressure for under investment in protective countermeasures.

2. Timely delivery of response measures is sometimes beyond the ability of current science and technology, or beyond the current capacities of human resources, production and sourcing of goods.

3. Obstacles to international co-operation and co-ordination often arise that impede implementation of countermeasures over a sufficiently large geographical scope to stem a shock.

Policy options

- Surveillance and early warning should be emphasised as a cost-effective measure of damage reduction and enabler of containment activities.

- A holistic review of prevailing incentive structures is needed to identify where and how production of protective countermeasures to systemic threats has been undermined, and policy makers should consider what fiscal and regulatory options are available to address such market failures.

- An inventory of strategic reserves and stockpiles of critical resources should be conducted as part of an assessment of resilience to global shocks.

- The design and implementation of complex systems should provide for early monitoring of future developments that could pose potential risks, and forward assessment for loss of control points on an ongoing basis.

Bibliography

Anderson, R. Boehme, Clayton *et al.* (2008), *Security Economics and the Internal Market*, available at *www.enisa.europa.eu/act/sr/reports/econ-sec/economics-sec*. Last accessed 17 December 2010.

Andersen, C.E., L. Bøtter-Jensen and E. Funck *et al.* (2000), "An International Intercomparison of National Network Systems used to Provide Early Warning of a Nuclear Accident Having Transboundary Implications", *Oxford Journals, http://rpd. oxfordjournals.org/content/92/1-3/89.short*, accessed 16 March 2011.

Anderson, R. and T. Moore (2006), "The Economics of Information Security", *Science 27*, Vol. 314, pp.610-613.

Asghari, H. (2010), "Botnet mitigation and the role of ISPs: A quantitative study into the role and incentives of Internet Service Providers in combating botnet propagation and activity", Delft University of Technology, Delft.

Ashford, W. (2010), "Cyber Europe 2010 proves successful stress test for public bodies", 10 November, *www.computerweekly.com/Articles/2010/11/10/243874/Cyber-Europe-2010-proves-successful-stress-test-for-public.htm*, accessed 22 March 2011.

Auf der Heide, E. (1989), *Disaster Response: Principles of Preparation and Coordination*, *http://orgmail2.coe-dmha.org/dr/pdf/DisasterResponse.pdf*

Back, E., A. Beith and R. Nugent (2010), "The race against drug resistance", The Centre for Global Development, Washington, DC.

Bank for International Settlements Communications (2010), "The Basel Committee's response to the financial crisis: report to the G20", Bank for International Settlements, Basel.

Beckman, D., Menkhoff, L., Sawischlewski, K. (2006), "Robust lessons about practical early warning systems", *Journal of Policy Modelling 28*, pp. 163-193.

Belke, A., A. Rees (2009), "The Importance of Global Shocks for National Policymakers – Rising Challenges for Central Banks", *Deutsches Institut für Wirtschaftsforschung Discussion Papers*, No. 922, Berlin.

Berkeley III, A.R. *et al.* (2010), "A Framework for Establishing Critical Infrastructure Resilience Goals, Final Report and Recommendations by the Council", National Infrastructure Advisory Council, October 19, *www.dhs.gov/xlibrary/assets/niac/niac-a-framework-for-establishing-critical-infrastructure-resilience-goals-2010-10-19.pdf*, accessed 22 March 2011.

Berg, A., E. Borensztein and C. Pattillo (2005), "Assessing Early Warning Systems: How have they worked in Practice?, *IMF Staff Papers*, Vol. 52, No. 3.

Bogdan, Thomas J. (2010), "State of the Space Weather Prediction Center 2010," presentation given at the Space Weather Prediction Center, Space Weather Workshop, Boulder, Colorado, 27-30 April.

Bauer, J.M. and M.J.G. van Eeten (2008), "Economics of Malware: Security Decisions, Incentives and Externalities", *STI Working Paper 2008/1*, Directorate for Science, Technology and Industry, OECD, Paris.

Briceno, S. (2007), "Global Early Warning Systems Needed", *United Nations Chronicle*, No. 2, quarterly, United Nations Department of Public Information, New York.

Bronner, G. and E. Géhin (2010), *L'Inquiétant principe de précaution*, Paris, PUF.

Cars, O. *et al.* (2011), "The Global Need for Effective Antibiotics: Moving towards Concerted Action", *Drug Resistance Updates*, Elsevier Ltd.

CBO (Congressional Budget Office) (2011), *Report on the Troubled Asset Relief Program,* The Congress of the United States, Washington, DC.

Clark, G.L. and R. Urwin (2007), *Best-Practice Investment Management: Lessons for Asset Owners from the Oxford-Watson Wyatt Project on Governance*, Oxford University Centre for the Environment, Oxford.

CENTRA Technology (2010), *Future Global Shocks Case Study: Geomagnetic Storms*, OECD, Paris.

Cooper, D. and A. Robertson (2007), "Disaster surge planning in Australia: measuring the immeasurable", *The Medical Journal of Australia, www.mja.com.au/public/ issues/186_08_160407/rob10218_fm.htm*l, accessed on 15 March 2011.

Congressional Budget Office (2009), CBO Report: The Troubled Asset Relief Program: Report on Transactions Through December 31, 2008, *www.cbo.gov/ftpdocs/99xx/ doc9961/01-16-TARP.pdf*, last accessed 5 January 2010.

Dessouky, M. and F. Ordonez (2008), *Supply Chain Management of the Strategic National Stockpiles,* Center for Risk and Economic Analysis of Terrorism Events, University of Southern California.

Evans, K. and F. Reeder (2010), *A Human Capital Crisis in Cybersecurity*, Center for Strategic and International Studies, *http://csis.org/files/publication/101111_Evans_ HumanCapital_Web.pdf*, last accessed on 20 November 2010.

European Commission (2009), *Report on Cross-border e-Commerce in the EU*, SEC (2009) 283 final, European Commission, Brussels, p. 5.

European Network and Information Security Agency (2010), "Interim findings of Cyber Europe 2010; a successful cyber stress test for Europe", 10 November, *www.enisa. europa.eu/media/press-releases/cyber-europe-2010-a-successful-2019cyber-stress-test2019-for-europe*, accessed 22 March 2011.

Fidler, D. (2010), "Negotiating Equitable Access to Influenza Vaccines: Global Health Diplomacy and the Controversies Surrounding Avian Influenza H5N1 and Pandemic Influenza H1N1", Indiana, *www.plosmedicine.org/article/info:doi/10.1371/journal. pmed.1000247*, accessed on 15 March 2011.

Fry, R. (2010), "Fighting Wars in Cyberspace", *The Wall Street Journal*, 21 July, Dow Jones and Company, New York.

Government of Canada, Office of Critical Infrastructure Protection and Emergency Preparedness (2002), *Threat analysis: Geomagnetic storms – Reducing the threat to critical infrastructure in Canada.*

Helmbrecht, U. (2010), *Interim findings of CYBER EUROPE 2010; a successful cyber stress test for Europe,* the European Network and Information Security Agency, Brussels.

International Monetary Fund (April, 2011), *World Economic and Financial Surveys Global Financial Stability Report, Durable Financial Stability: Getting There from Here,* available at *www.imf.org/external/pubs/ft/gfsr/2011/01/pdf/text.pdf.*

International Monetary Fund (10 January 2011), *IMF Performance in the Run-Up to the Financial and Economic Crisis: IMF Surveillance in 2004-07,* available at *http://imf-ieo. org/eval/complete/pdf/01102011/Crisis_Report_English.pdf, accessed 2 March 2011.*

International Monetary Fund (January 2011), IMF Factsheet: *The Financial Stability Assessment Programme,* available at *www.imf.org/external/np/exr/facts/fsap.htm,* accessed 2 February 2011.

Jianping, S. and G. Yu (2010), "A Study on KLR Financial Crisis Early-Warning Model", Higher Education Press and Springer-Verlag, Beijing.

Johnsen, E. and DiFiore, M. (2010), "To Be (Uniform) or Not To Be (Uniform)—That is the Question", *Traders Magazine Online News,* available at www.tradersmagazine. com/news/flash-crash-circuit-breaker-sec-finra-clearly-erroneous-trades-106201-1. html?zkPrintable=true, accessed 28 march, 2011.

Karl, K., Frey, A. (2010) "Striking the right balance: Insurance and Systemic risk regulation", *Swiss reinsurance Company Ltd.,* Zurich.

Lundstedt, H. (2006), "The Sun, Space \Weather and GIC Effects in Sweden," *Advances in Space Research* 37:6, publisher, place of publication.

Mehta, N. (2011), "Exchanges Revamp U.S. Curbs to Limit Stock Moves Instead of Halting Trades", *Bloomberg,* 6 April 2011.

Molinski, Tom S. *et al.* (2000), "Shielding Grids from Solar Storms," *IEEE Spectrum,* November 2000.

Murtagh, B. (2007), "Predicting and Mitigating the Effects of Space Weather: A Global Challenge", presentation given at the CDI/CSDS Conference, London, October 2007.

NAS (National Academy of Sciences) (2008), *Severe Space Weather Events-Understanding Societal and Economic Impacts Workshop Report,* National Academies Press, Washington, DC.

Nederberg F. *et al.* (2011) *Biodegradable nanostructures with selective lysis of microbial membranes,* Nature Publishing Group, United Kingdom.

Partridge J. (2010), "Global Production of Seasonal and Pandemic (H1N1) Influenza Vaccines in 2009-2010 and Comparison with Previous Estimates and Global Action Plan Targets", *World Health Organization H1N1 Influenza Vaccine Task Force,* Vol. 28, pp. 4 709-4 712.

Pulkkinen, Antti *et al.* (2010), "Solar Shield: Forecasting and Mitigating Space Weather Effects on High-Voltage Power Transmission Systems," *Natural Hazards* 53, Springer.

Rubin, H. (2010), *Future Global Shocks: Pandemics,* OECD, Paris.

Serritella, D. (2010) "High speed trading begets high speed regulation: sec response to flash crash, rash", *Journal of Law, Technology and Policy*, University of Illinois, Urbana-Champaign.

Sommer, P. and I. Brown (2010), *Reducing Systemic Cybersecurity Risk*, OECD, Paris.

Stewart, F. and J. Yermo (2008), "Pension Fund Governance: Challenges and Potential Solutions", Working Paper*s on Insurance and Private Pensions*, No. 18, OECD, Paris.

Teisberg, T. and R. Weiher (18 March 2009), Background Paper on the Benefits and Costs of Early Warning Systems for Major Natural Hazards, The World Bank Group Global Facility for Disaster Reduction and Recovery, accessed 15 March 2011, *www.gfdrr.org/gfdrr/sites/gfdrr.org/files/New%20Folder/Teisberg_EWS.pdf*

The Government Accountability Office (GAO) (2010), *Cybersecurity: Key Challenges Need to Be Addressed to Improve Research and Development*, GAO, Washington, DC.

Thomson Reuters (2010), "Factbox: Methodology used for EU bank stress test", July.

Thurner, S. (2010), *Agent-Based Models: Understanding the Leverage Cycle on National Scales*, OECD, Paris.

UN/ISDR (United Nations Inter-Agency Secretariat of the International Strategy for Disaster Reduction, Briceno, S. (2007) (2006), "Global Survey of Early Warning Systems Needed", United Nations Chronicle No. 2*: An assessment of capacities, gaps and opportunities toward building a comprehensive global early warning system for all natural hazards,* UN, Geneva.

United States Department of Homeland Security (2010), "Cyber Storm III – Federal Internet Stress Test Underway", 27 September, Washington, DC., *http://newsroom-magazine.com/2010/governance/cyber-storm-iii-federal-internet-stress-test-underway*, accessed 22 March 2011.

Eeten van, M.J.G.and J. M. Bauer (2008), "Economics of malware: Security Decisions, Incentives and Externalities STI working paper 2008/1 Information and Communication Technologies", Directorate for Science, Technology and Industry, OECD, Paris.

Wegener, H. (2007), "Qui se charge de maîtriser les dangers du cyberespace ?", *Forum du désarmement: les technologies de l'information et la sécurité internationale*, No. 3, Institut des Nations Unies pour la recherche sur le désarmement (UNIDIR), Geneva.

World Bank (2008), "A Regional Review", *World Bank* Working Paper No. 151: Weather and Climate Services in Europe and Central Asia", Washington, DC., *www.wmo.int/pages/prog/dra/eur/documents/DRRSEE%20Project/Weather%20and%20Climate%20Services%20in%20ECA%20June%202008.pdf*, accessed 15 March 2011.

World Health Organization (2001), "WHO Global Strategy for Containment of Antimicrobial Resistance Executive Summary", *http://whqlibdoc.who.int/hq/2001/WHO_CDS_CSR_DRS_2001.2a.pdf*, accessed 30 March 2011.

World Health Organization (2006), *Global pandemic influenza action plan to increase vaccine supply*, WHO, Geneva.

World Meteorological Organization (2011a), WMO monitoring meteorological conditions in quake-hit area, Press Release No. 909. *http://www.wmo.int/pages/mediacentre/press_releases/pr_909_en.html*.

Annex 4.A1

Comparative characteristics of routine emergencies/ disasters/ global shocks

Routine emergencies	Disasters	Global Shocks
Scale is modest and well-defined in space and time	Scale may be large, but defined	Scale is large and perhaps ill-defined in space and time. High impact possibly irreversible
Event recognised, but low visibility	High visibility	Very high profile, intense and long-lasting political and media interest
Interaction with familiar faces	Interaction with unfamiliar faces	Counterparts unknown
Familiar tasks and procedures	Tasks and procedures sometimes unfamiliar	Tasks and procedures outside previous experience
Intra-organisational co-ordination needed	Intra- and inter-organisational co-ordination needed	Multi-layered international co-ordination needed
Roads, telephones and facilities intact	Roads may be blocked or jammed telephones jammed or non-functional, facilities may be damaged	Transport and communication hubs blocked, ports may be damaged (airports, Internet ports, maritime ports), disrupting global supply chains
Communications frequencies adequate for radio traffic	Radio frequencies and mobile services often overloaded	International telecommunications overloaded or disrupted
Communications primarily intra-organisational	Need for inter-organisational information-sharing	Need for international information-sharing
Use of familiar terminology in communicating	Communication with persons who use different terminology	Communication between persons with different language, culture, norms and geo-political perspective
Need to deal mainly with local press	Hordes of national and international reporters	Media sources incapacitated, social media unmanageable
Management structure adequate to co-ordinate the number of resources involved	Resources often exceed management capacity	Resources sometimes cannot be accessed for long periods

Sources: left and centre columns are adapted from Auf Der Heide (2000); top 2 rows are adapted from Handmer and Dower (2007).

Chapter 5

Strategic approaches for managing future global shocks

Measured at the macro level, many if not most countries have been reaping the economic benefits of global economic integration, but there is a tendency to turn a blind eye to new vulnerabilities that result. Complex systems in the modern risk landscape contain various vulnerabilities to shocks that can result in rapid and widespread negative spillovers. Such broad exposure draws attention to the need for strategic preparation and international co-operation to support prevention and surveillance. This chapter considers elements of a strategic blueprint to better manage the known and unknown vulnerabilities that could produce global shocks. The key elements of the strategy include strengthening governance capacities through international institutions and norms, and building societal resilience. Each of these elements involves various components such as enhancing governance through the use of public-private partnerships, adapting risk communication to modern society and the use of new technologies, and improving the capacity of insurance solutions to enable rapid recovery.

Introduction

The past 30 years have seen transformative change in the risk landscape due to economic, social and technological drivers of interconnectedness, *e.g.* the integration of global markets, accelerated concentration of populations and assets, and rapid and inexpensive communications and travel. The flow of ideas and capital around the world can be almost immediate. As speed in communications and travel becomes less expensive, the significance of distance between people and events is altered by new opportunities and new vulnerabilities. On the one hand the globally integrated economy has enabled impressive productivity gains, bolstered international trade and foreign investment, and raised living standards in many countries. On the other hand it is built on greater interconnections, and in some cases interdependencies, that pave the path for more localised shocks to propagate and become events of global consequence. The challenge for policy makers is to preserve the gains that interconnectedness leads to, while managing the vulnerabilities.

The previous chapters illustrate international and national efforts to assess, map, model, monitor and protect against future global shocks. The speed at which vulnerabilities can become liabilities in this environment highlight the need for strategic preparation, thus this chapter considers elements of a strategic blueprint to better manage vulnerabilities. In some cases vulnerabilities in complex systems are known, but institutional and normative capacities are inadequate to support the capabilities needed to address them, especially when time constraints are tight. In other cases, vulnerabilities are surrounded by various uncertainties; *e.g.* with regard to the strength of connections or reliance of one critical system upon another. In cases where there are insufficient data and no model, scenario analysis can be useful to guide priorities in building societal and economic resilience; the capacity to adapt and return to a situation of near normalcy. The first section of this chapter considers how to enhance capacities to manage vulnerabilities via international co-operation and its complements. The second section focuses on the need to foster resilience through business continuity, risk communication and facilitating quick recovery.

Scaling-up capacities through improved international co-operation

Governance requires rules to regulate behaviour that creates negative externalities, and institutions to monitor and build capacity to adhere to the rules. Despite a growing recognition that global shocks will continue to happen, governance of such risks has not kept pace with the scale of potential consequences. The 2008 financial crisis exposed weaknesses in specific components of governance in the financial system, *e.g.* corporate boards, regulators and credit-rating agencies, but it also underscored the need for internationally co-ordinated policy responses to systemic risk in financial markets. This section considers gaps in institutions and norms to govern potential sources of global shocks. From this analysis a picture emerges of states playing continuing to play a key role in governance to prevent and responds to global shocks. It reflects upon the capacities that international co-operation should deliver and outlines a paradigm for future co-ordinated efforts. Attention is paid to the growing importance of non-state actors, who will increasingly be called upon to complement states in specific facets of governance gaps.

Institutional pillars for governance of future global shocks

To build governance capacities for global shocks requires reliable international partnerships. Institutional frameworks for these partnerships remain largely the domain of multilateral organisations, but a new order is emerging that gives increasing weight to the strategies of emerging economies, regional organisations, professional networks and Public Private Partnerships (PPPs). Regardless of the institutional structure adopted, organisations tend to co-operate only once two basic conditions are fulfilled. First, they must trust that information shared will not be used to their own prejudice. Second, the relationship must establish credibility in its capacity to collect, analyse, communicate and manage information relevant to a particular risk.

Table 5.1 is a non-exhaustive overview of national and international organisations with functions ranging from regulatory enforcement and policy or standard setting to data and information exchange. It illustrates the types of operational and policy-oriented bodies at national level that should co-operate with foreign counterparts and multilateral institutions to build capacity for the assessment, preparation and rapid response to risks with potential to propagate into global shocks.

Table 5.1. **Examples of institutions and networks that govern potential global shocks**

Global shock	National		International	
	Operational	Policy-oriented	Operational	Policy-oriented
Cyber risks	National CERT/ CSIRT Canadian CIRC French ANSSI Netherlands GOVCERT.NL Singapore IDA UK CSOC US CERT	Legislatures State ministries, departments and agencies	FIRST IMPACT/GRC NCIRC APCERT ENISA OAS INTERPOL NATO	OECD ITU Council of Europe APEC ENISA
Financial crises	Financial market regulators	Central banks Treasury ministries	IMF, FSB	G20, IMF, OECD, BCBS, IAIS, IASB, IOSCO, CPSS, CGFS
Pandemics	CDC	Health ministries	ECDC WHO/ GOARN	WHO
Geomagnetic Storms	NOAA NASA	–	ESA	–

What is the current capacity for governance of global shocks for pandemics, financial crises, cyber risks and geomagnetic storms? Taken together, the institutions with mandates to respond to these risks reflect a loosely knit patchwork of international co-operation between multilateral organisations, State bodies, non-governmental and quasi-public organisations. In the most formal of arrangements, multilateral organisations and treaties enshrined in public international law have been established to meet regularly and make decisions under previously established rules. But global governance also includes various informal networks and agreements used to scale up and enhance the effectiveness of responses to events that surpass the capacity of any one country to manage. Nonetheless, capacity gaps persist in the effort to address threats of recognised global importance. A cursory review of Figure 5.1 leads to the conclusion that the efforts to govern such rapid onset, high-impact events face significant deficits.

Figure 5.1. **Institutionalised monitoring capacity for global shocks**

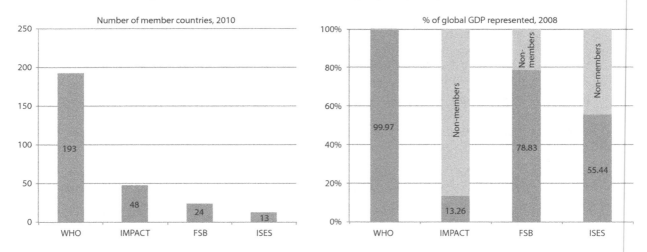

Source: (**left**) data compiled from WHO; IMPACT; FSB; ISES websites; (**right**) GDP data provided by EconStats. Global percentage calculations: OECD (2011).

Figure 5.1 only begins to scratch the surface as to why the World Health Organization (WHO) stands out as the most firmly established international institution in the realm of risk governance, with near universal membership and capacity to co-ordinate a global surveillance network for infectious diseases. The need to counter pandemics with co-ordinated, international action enjoys nearly unanimous support for obvious reasons. First, infectious diseases directly threaten what people tend to value most; their health. Second, there is a longer collective history of suffering from pandemics than from financial crises and cyber risks. Both these factors weigh heavily upon perceptions of risk. For all its success, WHO is a rich source of lessons on the complexities of governing global shocks, and it illustrates the scale of resources required to carry out a global mission effectively.

In the wake of the 2008 financial crisis, the G20 was expected to agree to design better rules for the conduct of finance, provide a new international financial architecture and reform global governance. Reform of the institutional landscape for international co-oper-ation in economic and financial issues is moving ahead slowly, although the G20 does not explicitly include an institution through which the multilateral perspective is brought to the table. The G20 thus shares at least one of the deficiencies of the system that it is expected to improve: a lack of impartial input into the discussion of global economic policy problems. The IMF provides much needed input to the discussions, but it does so effectively under the direction of the same governments that also sit in the G20. The Financial Stability Board (FSB) identifies key weaknesses underlying financial turmoil, and recommends actions to improve market and institutional resilience, but it only has 24 Member countries and it has no authority to issue binding directives, merely recommendations for action. The lack of an institution in possession of the information, expertise and impartiality that would enable it to swiftly identify and frankly communicate emerging risks to the global financial system and the world economy is a major governance gap.

International co-operation in the governance of global shocks seems to be proceeding in increments via bilateral, regional and multi-lateral initiatives. The immediate benefit of such arrangements is to provide a stable clearing house through which national bodies can communicate according to established protocols, to notify each other of an event rather than issuing conflicting reports to their populations and eventually to co-ordinate responses. There is no global intermediary to ensure the gathering and aggregation of surveillance data for all hazards from local and national bodies according to common standards and terminology. Such an organisation would be useful to perform analysis of trends and correlations that reveal vulnerabilities that are difficult to spot arising from cross-sectorial interconnections, and to distribute the results to help inform the national policy decisions of international partners. An even higher level of co-operation would involve the organisation of joint simulations and training, produce early warnings and develop plans for co-ordinated countermeasures at strategic junctures or control points that prevent or limit the contagion effects of global shocks. When warranted, a multilateral institution could be used as a forum to reach co-ordinated decisions to ensure consistent practice is implemented at national level.

Role of non-state actors in the governance of global shocks

An increasing number of non-state actors, such as standard-setting organisations, NGOs and Public-Private Partnerships, contribute to the improvement of capacities to manage issues of global consequence. It is expected that such complements to global governance will increasingly deliver specific improvements in risk assessment, early warning and response capacities, but not substitute the role of states (see Box 5.2). In many OECD countries upwards of 80% of critical infrastructures are operated by the private sector, and this is unlikely to change in the medium-term future. This rules out direct state control of the security of communications infrastructures and the information systems upon which power and water utilities, healthcare providers and others are critically dependent. Private operators have incentives to maintain continuity of service to their customers, but without some government intervention they may not be willing to commit resources to protecting such wider interests of society as public confidence in the availability of basic services (Sommer and Brown, 2010).

Governments can facilitate partnerships with critical infrastructure operators to share best practice, threat updates and analysis, and data on attacks. As a last resort after a catastrophic event, government agencies may need to take direct control over the operation of

---

Box 5.1. **Regional joint exercises in cybersecurity**

The first ever pan-European cyber attack simulation exercise was held in 2010 as a cyber stress test for readiness to face online threats to essential critical infrastructure. The event was organised by EU member states with support from the European Network Security Agency (ENISA) and the Joint Research Centre. All EU countries, as well as Iceland, Norway and Switzerland, took part either as active participants or observers. Although initially it was found that the exercise met its objectives, there was a lack of pan-European preparedness measures to test because many member states are still refining their national approaches to cyber attacks. In the interim findings on the exercise, EU member states agreed on the importance of involving the private sector in further exercises and sharing information on lessons learned with similar cyber test initiatives across the world. The interim report emphasised that the exercise was only the first step towards building pan-European trust and that more co-operation and information exchange was needed. The exercise highlighted the fact that incident-handling in different countries varies a lot because of the different roles, responsibilities and bodies involved in the process. The interim report said a pan-European directory of contacts should be updated regularly and member states should have greater understanding of how other EU countries manage cyber incidents.

critical information infrastructures using emergency powers. However, agencies will only be able to manage such complex, highly technological systems with close industry assistance (Sommer and Brown, 2010). Action taken before such events to increase infrastructural resilience is highly preferable to more direct intervention after a disaster has occurred. One route to exploring these issues is to devise war games specifically designed to reveal the tensions between government and private-sector entities, as opposed to the more usual aim of determining the overall level of damage likely to be sustained in a particular scenario.

Governments can use legislation, licensing and regulation to impose standards for security and resilience upon operators of critical infrastructure. This should become a core concern for regulatory agencies in the water, power, telecommunications, financial services and healthcare sectors. Just as has become common in the financial industries, regulators should conduct regular "stress test" exercises to measure vulnerabilities and ensure the resilience of infrastructure in the face of attack. Following the 2011 nuclear accidents in Japan, both the European Union and United States required nuclear operators to conduct so-called "stress tests" for reactors on their sites. Again it is important that these stress tests take place not only at the component level, but at the systemic level.

Box 5.2. **Global earthquake model**

Over half a million people have died since 2000 due to earthquakes, most of these in the developing world, where risk is increasing due to rapid population growth and urbanisation. The 2010-2011 earthquakes in Japan, New Zealand, Chile and Haiti illustrated once again the destructive impact of seismic events and the importance of the availability of reliable earthquake risk information. In many earthquake-prone regions no risk models exist to provide such information, and even where models do exist, they are often inaccessible, due to their proprietary nature or complex user-interface. Moreover, there are no agreed global standards for risk assessment, which are critical for effective and unambiguous communication of seismic risk. Reliable, uniform and consistent risk estimates for the entire world constitute critical input for increasing risk awareness and the undertaking of mitigating action. Such information is an essential puzzle piece for minimising loss of life, property damage and social and economic disruption due to earthquakes, by supporting decisions and actions that may lead to better building codes and construction, land-use planning for sustainable development, improved emergency response, protection of critical infrastructures and greater access to insurance. There is a need for this type of information to become accessible to a wide spectrum of organisations and individuals around the world. In response to this need, the Global Earthquake Initiative (GEM) aims to establish uniform, open standards to calculate and communicate earthquake risk worldwide, by developing a global, state-of-the-art and dynamic earthquake risk model together with exposed communities and ensuring it has understandable interfaces and tools for GEM's multitude of stakeholders.

Source: GEM (2011).

Certain facets of risk governance for cyber risks and geomagnetic storms, or space weather more generally, rely on such partnership arrangements. For example, partnerships between private and public bodies play an important role in the global space weather alerting system. By themselves, the alerts, warnings and watch documents issued by ISES through the SWPC are not always useful to industry consumers without additional analysis (FEMA, 2010). Air-travel dispatchers require decision support products providing analysis beyond SWPC alerts (American Meteorological Society, 2007). Private-sector entities take information from ISES as well as other sources and tailor it to the needs of specific industries, including utilities with transmission assets and pipeline operators. For instance, the Electric Power Research Institute combines space weather monitoring and prediction data from multiple sources and then performs its own economic impact analysis for its member utilities (Pulkkinen *et al.*, 2010). There is still much room for improvement in the realm of public-private partnerships. Private-sector entities have not emerged yet to provide full scope geomagnetic storm risk analysis for all critical infrastructure sectors. Service providers currently focus on warning satellite operators, utilities and pipelines. Second, the different public- and private-sector entities performing space weather monitoring and prediction services use different terminology; even within OECD member countries, different government agencies employ different terminology (American Meteorological Society, 2007). A standardised terminology would facilitate consumers' use of space weather monitoring and prediction information (FEMA, 2010).

Despite numerous disruptive worm and large-scale Distributed Denial of Service attacks over the past 25 years, the operational level of co-ordinated countermeasures to cyber risks does not measure up to what has been established for infectious diseases on a global level. To address this gap, the International Multilateral Partnership against Cyber Threats (IMPACT) was established as a public-private partnership in co-operation with the International Telecommunications Union (ITU). IMPACT aims to enhance global capacity to prevent, defend against and respond to cyber threats. Its focus is on assisting partner countries, and in particular on developing countries, in broadening their cybersecurity capabilities and capacity. IMPACT hosts the Global Response Centre (GRC), which aspires to become the foremost cyber threat resource centre in the world, *inter alia*, by providing the global community with a real-time aggregated early warning system. The GRC was built to play a pivotal role in realising the ITU's objective of putting technical measures in place to combat new and evolving cyber threats, but for the time being its membership is quite small.

Normative arrangements for governance of future global shocks

Institutional infrastructure is only one enabling pillar of effective governance. Normative arrangements such as treaties, legislation, standards, memoranda of understanding and codes of conduct contain incentives to undertake specific activities, such as vulnerability assessments and the exchange of surveillance and monitoring data and information. Incentives may include protective services, licensing, certification, eligibility for subsidies and access to information that enables an organisation to reinforce its own resilience. In certain cases, normative arrangements may provide for the possibility of levying sanctions upon parties for failure to comply with their terms. While a complete absence of norms is rare, reliance on ineffective norms is one of the main deficiencies in risk governance and was a key contributor to the global spread of risks. Table 5.2 provides examples of international and national normative arrangements relevant to the risk management of events that could potentially provoke global shocks.

Table 5.2. **Normative arrangements**

Global shock	International	National
Cyber risks	Convention on Cyber Crime; OECD Information Security Guidelines	Implementing provisions National Cybersecurity Plans
Financial crises	Compendium of Standards European Financial Stability Fund	Financial regulations, currency controls
Pandemics	International Health Regulations	National Influenza Pandemic Plans

Over the past decade sophisticated national and international pandemic planning has been widely put in place, and was broadly tested in the 2009-10 pandemic of novel H1N1 virus. Universal concern over pandemics has also led to the development of the International Health Regulations (IHR), which place binding obligations upon WHO Member countries to notify the WHO of any event which may constitute a public health emergency of international concern. Established guidelines assist member states to decide whether to notify WHO. For example, any case of human influenza caused by a new sub type must be reported. The IHR also set out core requirements for infectious disease surveillance, public alert and response. The public concern over infectious disease is also reflected in the initiatives of some regional institutions and their normative arrangements. Under European law, EU member states are required to notify the European Commission and each other via the Communicable Diseases Early Warning and Response System when infectious disease threats have public health implications for other member states.

The Financial Stability Board has put forth a "Compendium of Standards", which lists the various economic and financial standards that are internationally accepted as important for sound, stable and well-functioning financial systems (see Annex 5.A1). The international community attaches great importance to the adoption and implementation of these standards because of their beneficial effects on the stability of financial systems both inside countries and globally. The compendium highlights 12 *key standards which the FSB considers as deserving of priority implementation, taking account of* country circumstances. While the key standards vary in terms of their degree of international endorsement, they are broadly accepted as representing minimum requirements for good practice.

The Council of Europe Convention on Cybercrime (Cybercrime Convention) seeks to address computer crime and Internet crimes by harmonising national laws, improving investigative techniques and increasing co-operation among nations. Signatories to the convention are required to criminalise certain acts, *e.g.* violation of network security (including the production, sale, or distribution of unauthorised access tools). It also requires each signatory state to implement certain procedural mechanisms within their laws, for example law enforcement authorities must be granted the power to compel an Internet Service Provider to monitor a person's activities on line in real time. Finally, the Cybercrime Convention requires signatory states to provide international co-operation to the widest extent possible for investigations and proceedings concerning criminal offences related to computer systems and data, or for the collection of evidence in electronic form of a criminal offence. This means law-enforcement agencies have to assist police from other participating countries to co-operate with their mutual assistance requests.

Lax implementation of norms is a recurrent challenge in risk governance. Failure to execute standard safeguards constitute weak links that allow risks to grow and eventually spread beyond borders to endanger even those states and organisations that have made concerted efforts to protect themselves. In addition to the use of "off-the-shelf" cybersecurity solutions, both in public and private organisations, lax financial regulation and poorly implemented and resourced public health systems are well known weak links in global security. Norms may be adopted on the paper of a policy statement or legislation, but their utility is greatly diminished if they are not observed and go effectively unenforced. The mounting sophistication, frequency and severity of cyber attacks demonstrate the inefficacy of penalties such as incarceration and fines. This is expected to continue as long as cyber criminals know it is difficult to identify them, collect evidence of their activities, carry out an arrest and win a conviction.

Even where there is consensus about what norms to follow, risk governance needs to contend with the tendency of risks to constantly evolve in ways that overcome or sidestep controls. In their struggle for survival, viruses mutate and take on different characteristics of transmissibility, infectiousness and virulence; while in the search for the greatest return on investment, money is shifted to less stringently regulated financial regimes and actors. Hackers too have proven innovative in their ability to identify and exploit IT platforms, networks and software vulnerabilities. The ever-shifting nature of risks underscores the importance of institutions with sufficient authority to modify their agreed approaches and flexibility to adapt to their agreed norms in short order.

As this section illustrates, many normative arrangements have already been conceived to govern potential global shocks. Countries could make substantial progress by simply implementing what they have already agreed to do in terms of co-operating in the assessment, monitoring and response to global shocks. To encourage implementation, they could establish timetables, participate in an ongoing process of peer reviews and even submit themselves to penalties for non-compliance, but there seems to be little motivation to adopt any such tools of good governance.

Governance paradigm for future global shocks

In most OECD countries the well-known economic, environmental, technological and societal risks are governed by state institutions with varying degrees of co-operation from the private sector and input from civil society. Governance gaps may arise due to the absence or weakness of institutions, rules or capabilities that are necessary to effectively perform any of the following key functions of country risk management: risk identification and assessment of all hazards facing a country (its populations, assets and interests); surveillance and monitoring followed by timely and accurate reporting to produce situation awareness; operation of reliable early warning systems; development and implementation of prevention policies; establishment and execution of disaster response and recovery plans; enforcement of industrial safety and security regulations; and integration of lessons learned into each preceding phase.

Capacity to perform these key functions is generally developed with the intent to protect a country's domestic population and assets, but they may also be leveraged to bolster global governance capacities when they are insufficient to identify, manage or withstand shocks. International co-operation can help enhance governance of global shocks by enhancing three capacities in particular:

- Mapping of likely pathways to assess the vulnerability of system hubs with potential to propagate harmful consequences;

- Functional early warning systems that produce alerts about events of foreign origin with potential to exploit national vulnerabilities; and

- Planning and overseeing of rapid and proportionate responses to counter or control a shock before it propagates.

Figure 5.2 sketches the relationship between an internationally integrated mechanism for early warning and rapid response. Building cross-border capacity for early warning entails the expansion of national situation awareness to include risks that emerge abroad, and that hold potential to rapidly propagate across borders to impact upon national interests. It also requires the abilities to share, receive and integrate sources of information from partners abroad into risk assessments. The capacity for early warning should feed into the process of mounting a proportionate response via a co-ordinated decision-making process, which is also built on the ability to rapidly integrate services and equipment from foreign sources into the apparatus of countermeasures. This cannot realistically be achieved without protocols for mutual assistance and training drills.

Figure 5.2. **Key capacities for governance of future global shocks**

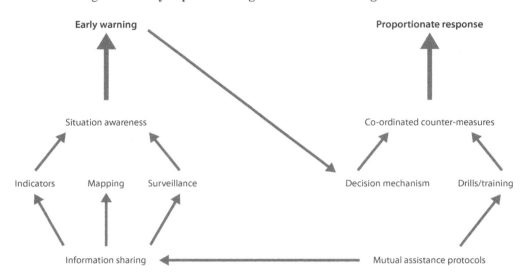

Outlook for governance of future global shocks

Given the gaps in institutions and rules overseeing international co-operation for management of global shocks, what prospect is there for improvement? As mentioned above, the global credit crisis is evidence that major governance gaps can lead to global shocks. As the financial architecture of the future must have an element that transcends national borders, so too must the governance of risks that could produce global shocks. Whether this takes the guise of a formal institution or informal network is only important if it impacts upon the efficiency and credibility of data-gathering and reporting that enable surveillance, early warning and rapidly co-ordinated response actions. Structured frameworks and ground rules for decision-making do tend to enable reliable international relations, however, and provide preferable conditions for co-operation between partners as opposed to ad-hoc arrangements.

International relations seem to be entering a particularly challenging period wherein the traditional global leaders are unable to agree on pressing issues with emerging powers, and between themselves. Even after the 2008 financial crisis G20 members disagree strongly about monetary and fiscal policy, exchange rates and global imbalances. They also differ on how to manage technology platforms, for example how open or controlled use of the Internet should be. While some countries argue that monitoring and authentication controls are necessary to ensure safe and secure use, others contend the impacts of such controls on e-commerce and freedom of speech are unacceptable trade-offs. Countries also differ on the modalities of technology transfer, with advocates for strong intellectual property regimes pointing to the positive spillovers of innovation in pharmaceutical products. Others countries argue in favour of making generic drugs immediately available to bolster weak public health systems. In violation of their agreed duties, some countries have even withheld epidemiological data about novel virus strains in the effort to secure an affordable price for vaccine that is eventually developed. For such reasons, co-operation between states seems to be breaking down when more than ever it needs to be strengthened.

Looking towards the future, a trend in the environment of risk governance is the increasing treatment of potential global shocks within the framework of national security doctrines. Many experts hold that pandemics and certain cyber attacks could be set off intentionally with economic impacts more akin to armed conflict than natural disasters, and argue for integrating military expertise to bolster prevention efforts and surge capacity for response as the logical next steps of integrated risk management. Clearly the military personnel in many OECD countries can contribute much-needed scientific and technological skills in this regard. Critics of this trend prefer stricter delineation between military defence and protection of civilian populations and assets. They contend that civilian police and public health workers are more familiar with protection of privacy and confidential information, and that a lack of trust between different national defence authorities is more likely to limit international co-operation to established alliances.

It is clear there is no one-stop institution for the governance of global shocks, but rather many international bodies with specialised mandates - much like the national ministries that tend to represent countries in these fora. At national level some countries have begun to address such silo operations by putting in place procedures for integrated risk management. This may involve horizontal reporting requirements on risks across ministries to an inter-ministerial co-ordinator or lead ministry. Alternatively it might entail a process to identify any interconnections with the broad range of risks facing the country (OECD, 2009). Without duplicating the progress that has been made to govern specific risks at international level, there is scope to reinforce the global capacity to identify risks that begin locally, but spread internationally, and to develop co-ordinated communication strategies and response plans in advance.

Building societal resilience to global shocks

The first section of this chapter lays out the institutional gaps in governance for global shocks, and suggests how international co-operation and partnerships between public and private actors can help to fill them. Policy makers need to assess the severity and likelihood of all identifiable risks facing their national territory and assets. This improves their position to target mitigation investments, finance redundancy in critical systems, and maintain diversification in critical systems through regulations. In addition to considering the full portfolio of economic, natural, social and technical risks, governments must also prepare to handle the unexpected. This section concentrates on strategic principles to ensure that society and critical systems can cope with risks that do occur. Its focus is not on prevention or protection, but rather on resilience. One of the main lessons to draw from recent extreme events is that no matter how prepared risk managers are, eventually some risks that have not been foreseen will happen, and therefore fostering resilience in society and its critical systems is required. Reinforcement involves actions on several fronts, including: identification of vulnerable populations and development of policies to ensure they can cope with adverse conditions; fortifying (or diversifying) critical infrastructure; adopting new technologies and adapting strategies for risk communication; and ensuring livelihoods based on money flows or the equivalent.

Identifying vulnerable populations

Social resilience refers to the capacity of a community (or organisation) to adapt under adverse conditions and restore a sense of normalcy from an external shock. The longer this takes, the more unlikely the community will ever fully recover its economic vitality, and the greater the risk of damage to the social fabric that holds it together. Efforts to foster resilience need to prioritise vulnerable populations (*e.g.* elderly, socio-economically disadvantaged, physically impaired people, people living in highly exposed housing). If a sufficient percentage of the vulnerable population is unable to cope with the effects of a shock event, the stress on social stability can reach a tipping point and lead to social unrest. It is important to identify socially vulnerable populations in advance, and provide for capabilities that reduce their vulnerability or bring them the aid they need when they need it. Although the focus here has been on people, similar reasoning supports the need to reinforce critical systems.

Social vulnerability research looks at the design of models which explain vulnerability (generally to environmental hazards) not just in terms of exposure and potential for monetary loss, but also the ability to recover. Since losses vary geographically, over time, and among different social groups, vulnerability also varies over time and space, hence the interest in the development of indicators and indexes to map vulnerability that reflect temporal and spatial variables (Villágran de León, 2006). Geographic Information Systems (GIS) are increasingly being used to map vulnerability, and to better understand

Figure 5.3. **Social vulnerability to environmental hazards**

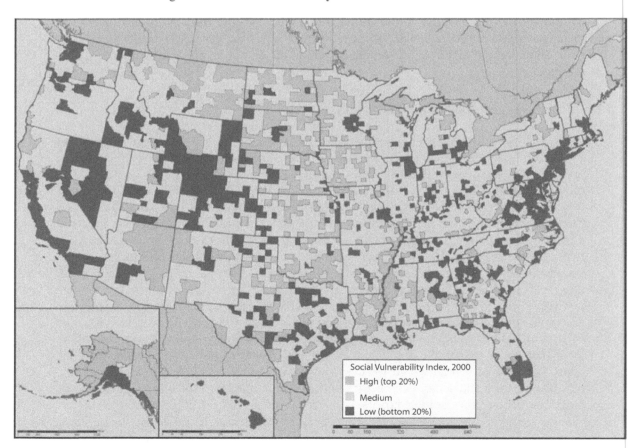

Source: Cutter (2001), available at *http://webra.cas.sc.edu/hvri/image/figure/sovi2000.png.*

how various phenomena (hydrological, meteorological, geophysical, social, political and economic) affect human populations. An even greater aspiration in social vulnerability research is the search for one, broadly applicable theory, which can be applied systematically on a variety of scales, all over the world.

One approach to quantifying a geographic locality's vulnerability to hazards is based on its underlying socioeconomic and demographic profile. A social vulnerability index (SoVI) compares several socio-economic factors to the national mean, including: personal wealth, age, density of built environment, single-sector economic dependence, housing stock and tenancy, race and ethnicity, occupation, and infrastructure dependence. The index is a sum of the deviation from the mean for each of the factors listed (Cutter, 2003). *Post mortem* studies indicate a strong relationship between the losses from natural hazards and the socio-economic levels of those most affected (CENTRA, 2010). A logical extension of this argument is that populations with higher socio-economic levels would be more likely to have the means and access to information to deal with effects from future global shocks. Figure 5.3 superimposes a social vulnerability index onto a map of the United States using census data from 2000, aggregates socio-economic factors and weighs them all equally. This index contains potential insights into the extent to which a major disruptive event will have an effect on the population of a region, with highly vulnerable groups most likely to exhibit behavioural changes or unrest.

Reinforcing resilience of businesses to shocks

The economic impacts of a global shock are likely to be severe for companies with worldwide operations, global supply chains and international customers, and for countries that rely on these companies for job creation and tax revenues. It is insufficient for firms to rely on government plans about what course of action they should take if prevention policies and countermeasures fail. Businesses and civil society must take it upon themselves to plan in advance to reduce the impacts of absenteeism due to employee illnesses or travel and power outages due to critical infrastructure disruptions. The impacts of policy responses such as restrictions on travel and trade, quarantines, school closures and bans on public gatherings may serve to isolate a virus or disruption, but they create obstacles to commerce that risk prolonging the phase of economic recovery to follow.

Once a disaster strikes it is too late to create effective plans to cover the fallout for production, employees, reputation, supply chains or service disruption. Contingency plans for a broad range of adverse event scenarios must be in place, and they must build in flexibility to account for unknowns that can generate extreme events. Regulators of the power, water and financial services industries typically require detailed continuity plans to be made and tested regularly, however mapping of the risks that transcend these sectors is still nascent.

Protecting the continuity of an organisation's mission or business is very difficult if its "mission critical" functions are not clearly identified. Managers need to understand their organisations from a broader point of view than the area they control and set priorities for ensuring their operations or a back-up plan as a contingency. A fully redundant capability for each function is prohibitively expensive for most organisations, so in the event of a disaster, certain functions will not be performed. If appropriate priorities have been set and approved by senior management, it could mean the difference in the organisation's ability to survive a global shock. Incorporating a risk management process to operations, such as ISO 31 000 or the IRGC risk management framework, can be instrumental in collecting the right evidence base for decisions about whether a system is critical to the organisation's mission and whether to increase robustness, redundancy and/or diversification of systems that have been identified.

Major volatility in agricultural prices over recent years has created uncertainty in food manufacturers' earnings, but companies could mitigate the impact by adopting measures beyond financial hedging instruments. Long term purchase arrangements that use a combination of fixed and indexed prices are an example of alternative ways to acquire supplies at a stable cost. Some food manufacturers are also training farmers to grow coffee and supplying them with coffee trees. To be effective, companies must simultaneously establish regular communication across departments ranging from procurement to treasury so that senior managers can evaluate if the organisation's entire range of commodity price risk management practices fits with its corporate objectives (Robson M and Wittenberg A., 2010).

In most major economies, the electricity sector is second only to ICT in terms of interconnectedness to other critical sectors. The strengths of some of its key connections, however, are even stronger than those of ICT's, *e.g.* as used in manufacturing, and of course modern ICT itself relies on electricity. This explains the importance of mitigating the supply chain vulnerabilities of the electricity sector. Extra-high-voltage transformers face numerous supply challenges, including: long manufacturing lead times, foreign production, high cost, highly customised designs, and difficult logistics (NIAC, 2010). Maintaining spare transformers at all locations is extremely costly, but some countries have created programmes that help utilities to share their inventory of spare transformers and mitigate sector risks. Additional options to improve supply include standardisation of transformer design, development of a recovery transformer, and incentives to encourage additional domestic manufacturing of extra-high-voltage transformers. Box 5.3 outlines the key elements of specific resilience measures for all sectors of critical infrastructure.

Box 5.3. **Key elements of resilience in critical infrastructure**

Robustness - The ability to keep operating or to remain standing in the face of disaster. In some cases, this entails designing structures or systems to be strong enough to take a foreseeable shock. In others, robustness requires devising substitute or redundant systems that can be brought to bear should something important break or stop working. Robustness also entails investing in and maintaining elements of critical infrastructure so that they can withstand low probability but high-consequence events.

Resourcefulness - The ability to skilfully manage a shock event as it unfolds. This includes identifying options, prioritising what should be done both to control damage and to begin mitigating it, and communicating decisions to the people who will implement them. Resourcefulness depends primarily on people, not technology.

Rapid recovery - The capacity to get things back to normal as quickly as possible after a disaster. Carefully drafted contingency plans, competent emergency operations, and the means to get the right people and resources to the right places are crucial.

Adaptability - The means to absorb new lessons that can be drawn from a catastrophe. It involves revising plans, modifying procedures, and introducing new tools and technologies needed to improve robustness, resourcefulness, and recovery capabilities before the next crisis.

Source: National Infrastructure Advisory Council, 2010.

Adapting risk communication to modern society and technologies

Risk communication plays a role in managing risks, and these roles need to be adapted to the needs of preparing for future global shocks. Before an event, risk managers need to raise public awareness about social vulnerabilities due to increased interdependencies in critical systems. This is not an easy task, but several countries recently published security policy documents clearly set out this context up front, *e.g.* the "White Paper on Defence and National Security" in France, and the "National Security Strategy" of the Netherlands and the "National Response Framework" of the United States. The United Kingdom has taken this effort one step further with the publication of the "National Risk Register", in which the government identifies many of the key risks facing the national territory.

When a global shock event occurs, or is about to occur, a main task for risk managers is to convey information and instructions related to preserving safety and supporting relief and recovery. Even where internationally recognised classifications for event-scales have been established (*e.g.* strength of earthquakes, pandemic phases, nuclear accidents, strength of solar flares) there is a tendency for local authorities to downplay the severity of some events to avoid a panic. Foreign sources have their own means to evaluate the situation, but often less data than the local sources. Their objective is to communicate risks to the people to whom they are ultimately accountable, and for whom cultural differences might require placing emphasis on different facts. Without a mechanism for international co-ordination, how foreign information sources reported an event may have important effects on how it is perceived in the country where the event emerges, despite what the authorities there say. Under these circumstances, the ability of risk managers to communicate effectively with their own population is sometimes pre-empted by foreign sources.

Failure to convince the public that it faces a genuine risk may have serious consequences. Thousands of people die every year from influenza-related illness, and hundreds of thousands more are hospitalised. Current policy in many OECD countries recommends that every person six months of age or older be vaccinated each year for seasonal flu. Voluntary vaccination programmes, however, have not proven to be very successful. During the 2008-09 H1N1 pandemic, the low level of vaccination rates in many countries indicated a failure of risk communication. In the United States, the Centers for Disease Control and Prevention (CDC) estimated that only 62% of healthcare professionals received the seasonal flu vaccine between August 2009 and January 2010, and only 35% also received the H1N1 swine flu vaccine.

In future, public officials need to clearly explain the relative benefit and risk of vaccines to the public, and their general safety should be emphasised. Since most vaccines have at least minor side-effects on some people, when regulatory approval is expedited the public has concerns that need to be addressed. Decision makers are often concerned that complete transparency will undermine compliance with their directives, but the flip-side is that a lack of transparency undermines public trust and willingness to follow directions at crucial times.

As communications technology evolves and diversifies, different populations (generations, socio-economic groups) converge around different media platforms (radio, television, Internet, social media). A diversity of communication channels should be used to ensure as many people as possible are warned of an impending event, to avoid failure of any one channel and to reinforce the warning message. It is also important to make use of the full range of available platforms to communicate a message to the public rapidly. Social media in particular enable users to create and sustain dialogue between individuals and networks – all the while passing information back and forth. Public authorities and the voluntary sector have begun to realise the potential of using social media to transmit information quickly, catalyse action and provide a mechanism for feedback at a relatively low cost (see Box 5.4).

Box 5.4. **Social media and risk communication 2.0**

Twitter made headlines when it was found that nearly 2% of all tweets globally made some reference to the 2009 influenza pandemic. The potential is vast for governments and voluntary organisations to use social media to communicate important messages and advice to the public. Twitter was the primary mode of communication for Iranian protestors in 2009 during the post-election violence. It enabled the world at large to stay abreast of the events there from the 140-character microblogs popularly known as status updates. Twitter was also used by trapped survivors in Haiti who used the service to direct rescue efforts using the *hashtag #rescuemehaiti*.

A notable tool for crowd sourcing in disaster management is Ushahidi. Developed during the Kenyan post-election violence to assist aid agencies in finding affected persons; Ushahidi is an open source project that allows information gathering via sms, email or web and visualises it on a map or timeline for crisis response. In Haiti for example it informed people where aid would be delivered and where aftershocks were reported.

Emergency management organisations are aware that Twitter follows a model of information flow that closely manages rumour-mongering. The spread of misinformation in social media is a concern that public officials should not ignore. An additional concern associated with the volume of information distributed by social media is that it can lead to false positives, confusing messages and actually ends up obscuring useful information. Hence the degree of its efficiency is still debatable.

All media sources, including television, Internet, print and radio media, are potential platforms for disseminating information that is essential to successful emergency management, but there is broad scope for conflicting messages to find their way into the public domain very quickly. Communication must be accomplished without comprising the clarity of the message or undermining the authority of its source. The public needs a single, credible voice to provide clear and accurate answers to questions that divergent sources may raise and to resolve any confusion. Formal pandemic declarations and alerts issued by governments in 2009 faced scepticism and achieved only limited success. In several OECD countries a vocal minority of medical doctors had publicly questioned the severity of the outbreaks and denounced state efforts at mass vaccination. While censorship of a media platform is not a policy option for democratic societies, holding individuals accountable for unprofessional behaviour is. Some governments have trained technical risk specialists (*e.g.* hydrological engineers) to conduct public relations during large scale disasters. These officials are trained to provide the media with sufficient details and scientific facts to substantiate the information reporters need to transfer an accurate and reliable message to the public, and to debunk pseudo-scientific arguments that in past have undermined public confidence.

Recent information and communication technologies hold significant potential to improve risk communication. Social media, for example, empowers the public to take active roles in gathering and transmitting information, which distinguishes it from the traditional model of risk communication. It enables people with direct information of an event to enrich decision-making by providing it in real time. Whereas broadcasting messages offers information to the public in the form of advice and guidance, social media changes that equation by inviting users to take part by sharing information with others, evaluating its reliability, even cross-referencing it with visual aids such as maps. This can prove crucial in the context of disaster management and emergency planning. The benefits of social media are not simply a matter of attracting the attention of individuals in younger generations who rely primarily on a news source, it can better provoke individuals to act on an official message, for example "Evacuate now by route A." The message also passes to the individual's network, which is crucial when important messages need to be spread swiftly. Social media may act as a real time feedback mechanism by enabling individuals and communities to share and co-operate with one another outside the framework of traditional institutions and organisations. Its advantages include self-policing and the generation of information that cannot otherwise be easily obtained.

Insurance as an enhancer of financial resilience

Without livelihoods based on flows of money or its equivalent, people cannot regroup or otherwise recover from a shock in a timely manner. Sources of flows include remittances, aid, asset sales and insurance. Remittances and aid often come from foreign locations, which might not be accessible after a global shock. Assets are valuable at such times only if they are sufficiently liquid to produce flows of money or goods and services. Insurance, therefore, is a key ingredient of financial resilience to global shocks. In 2008, natural catastrophes caused total losses of USD 270 billion worldwide, but less than 20% of this amount was insured (Swiss Re, 2009). In the face of an upswing in large-scale disasters over the past 40 years the insurance industry has generally demonstrated its capacity to handle massive claims for indemnification (Figure 5.4). Global shocks, however, might present challenges to the sufficiency of these reserves. Of the 25 most costly insured catastrophes in the past 40 years, two-thirds have occurred since 2001 (Kunreuther and Useem, 2010). What can be done to enable insurers to meet their obligations under the remote possibility that several disastrous events occur at or near the same time? How can claims be serviced in a timely manner if electricity, telecommunications and/ or transport systems do not function due to the shock event(s)?

Figure 5.4. **Rising number of catastrophic events**
Number of events 1970-2009

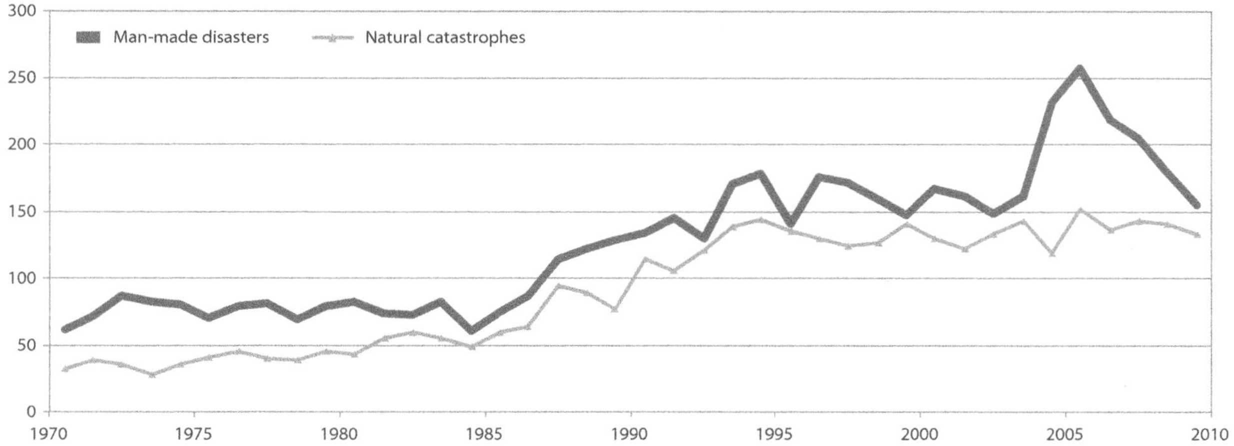

Source: Swiss Re (2011), "Natural catastrophes and man-made disasters in 2010" sigma No. 1/2011, Copyright © Swiss Re, available at *www.swissre.com/sigma/.*

The first of these challenges has been extensively examined for pandemic scenarios, which are thought to be capable of damaging profitability in the health, life and pension (re)insurance sectors for several years. The "natural hedge" against a rush of life insurance claims is that annuity payments may cease earlier than expected (due to premature death of the annuitant). This is not certain to be the case, as seen with the 1918 influenza pandemic, which primarily affected those of working age and was little worse than a "normal" winter flu for the elderly. During a severe pandemic a series of knock-on effects on the insurance industry are anticipated. There is concern that while capital may be adequate to withstand the rush of life insurance claims, payments may cease earlier than expected and the balance sheet of life and health re-insurers may be weakened at a time when property and casualty policy holders are also looking to make claims.

Industries that involve a significant amount of close interaction between humans such as entertainment, hospitals, hotels, travel and universities will be expected by third parties to have thought through the impact of pandemic fully and have robust and tested plans in place. Insurers may have to indemnify damages resulting from the negligence of such parties who do not plan adequately and put others at risk. The results of a survey of several hundred multi-national enterprises showed that over three-quarters of companies have inadequate plans for coping with a flu pandemic. Around one-third of businesses have no strategy at all, while 14% have only rudimentary contingency plans. Approximately one-third of executives are unaware of how their companies intend to deal with the threat, and only 22% are comfortable that they are prepared (Marsh, 2009).

Similarly, directors in companies that do not plan properly and suffer disproportionate financial losses when compared to their competitors may be sued for loss of shareholder value. A company with weak worker protection plans compared to their peers might be considered as having failed in their duty of care to employees. This may impact healthcare facilities disproportionately. Medical malpractice claims could dramatically increase given the potential for inadequate surge capacity. Claims involving the hotel and hospitality business interruption, event cancellation and travel disruption may increase.

A global recession is one possible result of a severe pandemic scenario. Many businesses will struggle with absenteeism; food shortages in many areas may occur if supply chains are affected. In the aftermath of natural disasters, sporadic looting often occurs until outside reinforcements can stabilise basic living conditions. If a deep recession has been triggered, there is a precedent for increases in fraudulent claims. Not only would the overwhelming flood of simultaneous claims test the ability of insurers to provide policy-holders with swift compensation, the general downturn in the economy could impact demand for insurance with a corresponding reduction of inflows from premium income while overheads remain. It is also important to note that while the impacts on different sectors identified above might not all be damaging issues on their own, taken together they will have a larger impact. This is an example of "tail dependency" that was witnessed in the aftermath of the 9/11 terrorist attacks; for very large-scale events, things tend to go wrong at the same time (Kousky and Cooke, 2009).

Global shocks can be expected in many cases to have similar consequences on local economies as natural disasters. The rising impact of disasters is driving up the costs of relief and reconstruction, and has well-documented, adverse impacts on development gains in the poorest of countries. In some countries private-sector insurers have offered innovative risk-transfer products to mitigate the financial impact of such events. These solutions provide models for governments and NGOs to manage disaster expenses more efficiently by funding them before – instead of after – a catastrophe occurs. Public-sector entities have the option to leverage their available funds through the use of capital market instruments, allowing governments to smooth and protect their budgets at lower opportunity costs and ensuring more adequate funds for relief activities (Swiss Re, 2008). The potential damages from future global shocks could be so high that strategic planning for recovery requires a fundamental rethink about how to expand the current global capacity of insurers. One proposal is to explore how to reinforce this capacity by easing access to the full depth of global capital markets.

Figure 5.5. **Insured catastrophe losses 1970-2009**

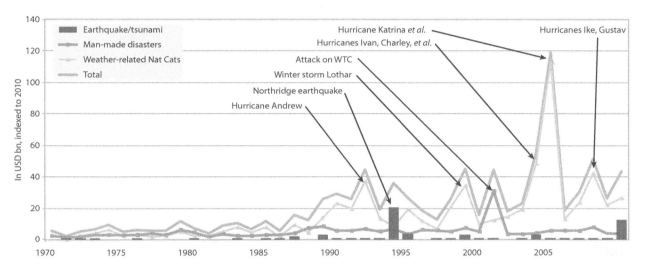

Source: Swiss Re (2011), "Natural catastrophes and man-made disasters in 2010", *Sigma* No. 1/2011, Copyright © Swiss Re, available at *www.swissre.com/sigma/*.

Conclusions

- States will continue to play a central role in management of global shocks, but they will increasingly need to act in concert with other actors, such as the corporate sector, NGOs, the scientific community and ordinary citizens.

- Due to their remote source, many known hazards cannot be easily prevented or regulated; the principal options are reactive capacities and resilience.

- Social vulnerability measurements can help direct efforts to build resilience capacity.

- Future global shocks can give rise to confusion or misunderstandings amongst the public as a result of divergent messages tailored to different audiences and cultures.

Policy options

- International co-ordination to address global shocks should be strengthened at all phases of the risk management cycle and in particular through the use of partnerships between public and private actors.

- Self-organisation needs to be promoted across society as a cornerstone of building resilience.

- Efforts to improve resilience should focus on routine processes, *e.g.* information-sharing, broad consultation and participation, training exercises and simulations, citizen level resilience.

- Internationally agreed information procedures could be expanded to co-ordinate announcements of global shocks, without prejudice for each country to convey an appropriate message to its populace.

Bibliography

American Meteorological Society Policy Program and SolarMetrics (2007), *Integrating Space Weather Observations & Forecasts into Aviation Operations,* American Meteorological Society & SolarMetrics Policy Workshop Report.

Briguglio, L., G. Cordina, N. Farrugia, and S. Vella (2005) "Conceptualizing and Measuring Economic Resilience", *Pacific Islands Regional Integration and Governance*, ANU Press, Canberra, pp. 26-49.

Diekmann, N. *et al.* (2008), *CRO briefing: Emerging Risks Initiative – Position Paper: The Digital Economy's Achilles heel*, Critical Information Infrastructure, Amstelveen.

Cabinet Office United Kingdom (2008), "The National Security Strategy of the United Kingdom Security in an Interdependent World", Crown Copyright, Surrey, *http://interactive.cabinetoffice.gov.uk/documents/security/national_security_strategy.pdf.*

Cabinet Office (2008), "National Risk Register", Crown Copyright, Surrey.

Casti, J. (2011), "Future Global shocks: Four Faces of Tomorrow", OECD, Paris.

CENTRA Technology (2011), "Future Global Shocks Case Study: Geomagnetic Storms", OECD, Paris.

Cooke, R.M.and C. Kousky (2009), "The Unholy Trinity: Fat Tails, Tail Dependence, and Micro-Correlation", Resources For the Future, Washington.

Dunn, M. (2007), "Critical Infrastructures: Vulnerabilities, Threats, Responses", CSS Analyses in Security Policy, Vol. 2, No. 16, Zurich.

FEMA (U.S. Federal Emergency Management Agency) (2010), *Managing Critical Disasters in the Transatlantic Domain – The Case of a Geomagnetic Storm Workshop Summary, February 23-24, 2010, Boulder, Colorado, U.S.A.*, Washington, DC, Government Printing Office.

Frey, A., M. Kirova, C. Schmidt (2009), "The role of indices in transferring insurance risks to the capital markets", *Sigma*, No. 4, Swiss Reinsurance Company, Zurich.

Global Earthquake Model (2011), Global Earthquake Model report 2009/2010, Second Edition, Pavia.

Gordon, L.A., M.P. Loeb and T. Sohail (2003), "A Framework for Using Insurance for Cyber Risk Management", Communications of the ACM, Vol. 46, No. 3, New York, pp. 81-85.

Gros, D., U. Klüh and B. Mauro. (2009), "Reforming Global Governance: How to Make the IMF More Independent", *Intereconomics*, Vol. 44, No. 2, pp.72-81.

Hapgood, M. (2010), "Space Weather: Its impact on Earth and Implications for Business", Lloyd's 360 Risk Insight, Lloyds, London.

HM Government (2010), "A Strong Britain in an Age of Uncertainty: The National Security Strategy", Crown Copyright, Surrey.

Kourilsky, P. and G. Viney (2000), *Le Principe de précaution : rapport au premier ministre*, Odile Jacob, La Documentation française.

Kunreuther, H. and M. Useem (2010), *Learning from Catastrophes: Strategies for Reaction and Response*, Pearson Education, New Jersey.

Marsh (2009), "H1N1 Influenza: Preparing for and Responding to a Pandemic", Pandemic Preparedness and Response, Vol. VI, Issue 1, *http://global.marsh.com/documents/ Marsh_Risk_Alert_H1N1_Influenza.pdf*, accessed 22 March 2010.

Mummert, A. and H. Weiss (2011), "Get the News Out Loudly and Quickly: Modelling the Influence of the Media on Limiting Infectious Disease Outbreaks", *http://arXiv.org*.

Murphy, D. (2010), *Improving the Resilience of Critical Infrastructure*, Cabinet Office, Crown Copyright, Surrey.

OECD (2009), *Innovation in Country Risk Management*, OECD, Paris.

Présidence de la République (2008), *The French White Paper on Defence and National Security*, Paris.

Pulkkinen, Antti *et al.* (2010), "Solar Shield: Forecasting and Mitigating Space Weather Effects on High-Voltage Power Transmission Systems", *Natural Hazards* 53.

Robson M., A. Wittenberg (2010), "Separating the Wheat from the Chaff: How volatile agricultural prices are rewriting the rules for the food industry", Corporate Risk, Olivier Wyman Group.

Rubin, H. (2011), "Future Global Shocks: Pandemics", OECD, Paris.

Sommer, P. and I. Brown (2011), "Reducing Systemic Cybersecurity Risk", OECD, Paris.

Mitchell, M. and R. Schnarwiler (2008), "Disaster risk financing: Reducing the burden on public budgets", Swiss Re Focus Report, Swiss Reinsurance Company Ltd, Zurich.

Swiss Re Focus Report (2009), "Country Risk Management: Making Societies More Resilient*", Swiss Reinsurance Company Ltd*, Zurich

Villagrán De León, J.C. (2006), "Vulnerability: A Conceptual and Methodological Review", *Publication Series of UNU-EHS*, No. 4, Bonn.

The Conservative Party (2010) "A Resilient Nation: National Security Green Paper", *Policy Green Papers*, No. 13, London.

The White House (2010), "National Security Strategy", May, *www.whitehouse.gov/sites/ default/files/rss_viewer/national_security_strategy.pdf*, accessed 22 March.

Thurner, S. (2011), "Agent Based Models: Understanding the Leverage Cycle on National Scales", OECD, Paris.

Weigle, B. (2007), "Prediction markets: another tool in the intelligence kitbag", *USAWC strategy research project*, Philadelphia.

Weisbart, S. (2006), "Pandemic: Can the Life Insurance Industry Survive the Avian Flu?", Insurance Information Institute, New York.

Zha, D. (2009), "Exogenous Shocks Such as Terrorism and Pandemics as a Threat to Regional Crisis Management", The Mansfield Foundation, Washington, DC.

Zurich (2008), "Dealing with the Unexpected: Lessons for Risk Managers from the Credit Crisis", Zurich Financial Services, Zurich.

Annex 5.A1

Compendium of Standards

Area	Standard	Issuing Body
Macro-economic policy and data transparency		
Monetary and financial policy transparency	Code of Good Practices on Transparency in Monetary and Financial Policies	IMF
Fiscal policy transparency	Code of Good Practices on Fiscal Transparency	
Data dissemination	Special Data Dissemination Standard/General Data Dissemination System	
Institutional and market infrastructure		
Insolvency	Insolvency and Creditor Rights	World Bank
Corporate governance	Principles of Governance	OECD
Accounting	International Accounting Standards (IAS)	IASB
Auditing	International Standards on Auditing (ISA)	IFAC
Payment and settlement	Core Principles for Systemically Important Payment Systems Recommendations for Securities Settlement Systems	CPSS CPSS/IOSCO
Market integrity	The 40 Recommendations of the Financial Action Task Force / Nine Special Recommendations Against Terrorist Financing	FATF
Financial regulation and supervision		
Banking supervision	Core Principles for Effective Banking Supervision	BCBS
Securities regulation	Objectives and Principles of Securities Regulation	IOSCO
Insurance supervision	Insurance Core Principles	IAIS

Source: Financial Stability Board: *www.financialstabilityboard.org/cos/key_standards.htm.*

Annex A

Glossary

Bot-infected computers	Networks of compromised computers that unknown to their owners run a malicious piece of software (called a bot). This code puts the computer under the control of a remote attacker, who then uses these bots to accomplish a variety of illegal tasks – from sending spam emails and disruption of the network, to identity and financial theft.
Complexity	Something with many parts in intricate arrangement. Complex is the opposite of independent, while complicated is the opposite of simple.
Complex system	A system composed of interconnected parts that as a whole exhibit one or more properties (behaviour among the possible properties) not obvious from the properties of the individual parts.
***Consequence**	The effect of an event, incident, or occurrence, commonly measured in four ways, human, economic, mission, and psychological, but may also include other factors such as impact on the environment.
***Criticality**	The importance to a mission or function, or to continuity of operations.
Distributed Denial of Service Attack	A form of cyber stack that involves saturating the target machine with external communications requests, such that it cannot respond to legitimate traffic, or responds so slowly as to be rendered effectively unavailable.
Emerging constructs	Major trends or new and persistent threads of behaviour driven by a particular alignment in incentives or a technological innovation.
External factors	Factors outside a system that have the potential to change it and cause events that could propagate through it.
***Hazard**	A natural or man-made source or cause of harm or difficulty.
Honey pot	A trap set to detect, deflect, or in some manner counteract attempts at unauthorised use of information systems. Generally it consists of a computer, data, or a network site that appears to be part of a network, but is actually isolated and monitored, and which seems to contain information or a resource of value to attackers.

Hubs	Nodes which are connected to a large number of other nodes within a system.
Interdependency	The strength of the link between elements in a system that are related in such a way that functionality of both can be affected by a single event.
***Likelihood**	The chance of something happening, whether defined, measured or estimated objectively or subjectively, or in terms of general descriptors (such as rare, unlikely, likely, almost certain), frequencies, or probabilities.
Map gaps	Areas where resources, infrastructures, networks, etc. are missing from a system.
***Mitigation**	An ongoing and sustained action – implemented prior to, during, or after an incident occurrence – to reduce the probability of, or lessen the impact of, an adverse incident.
Nodes	Components of a system which frequently, but not always, have connections to other components.
Pathways	A unidirectional link between two elements of a system in which one node is affected as a result of an event in another.
Risk governance	The totality of actors, rules, conventions, processes and mechanisms concerned with how relevant risk information is collected, analysed and communicated, and how and by whom management decisions are taken and implemented (IRGC, 2009).
***Risk management**	The process of identifying, analysing, assessing, and communicating risk and accepting, avoiding, transferring or controlling it to an acceptable level considering associated costs and benefits of any actions taken.
Scale-free networks	A network whose degree of distribution, *i.e.* the probability that a node selected uniformly at random has a certain number of links (degree), follows a power law.
***Scenario**	A hypothetical situation comprised of a hazard, an entity impacted by that hazard, and associated conditions including consequences when appropriate.
Scope	Determining the number of nodes and connections present within a complex system.
System	A set of interacting or interdependent system components forming an integrated whole.

*Threat	A natural or man-made occurrence, individual, entity, or action that has or indicates the potential to harm life, information, operations, the environment and/or property. For the purpose of calculating risk, the threat of an intentional hazard is generally estimated as the likelihood of an attack being attempted by an adversary; for other hazards, threat is generally estimated as the likelihood that a hazard will manifest.
*Vulnerability	A physical feature or operational attribute that renders an entity, asset, system, network, or geographic area open to exploitation or susceptible to a given hazard; a qualitative or quantitative expression of the level to which an entity, asset, system, network, or geographic area is susceptible to harm when it experiences a hazard.
Zero-day cyber-attacks	The exploit of a vulnerability in an information system that is created before, or on the same day as the vulnerability is learned about by its vendor. By creating a virus or worm that takes advantage of a vulnerability the vendor is not yet aware of and for which there is not currently a patch available the attacker can wreak maximum havoc.

Note: * indicates the term was taken from the United States Department of Homeland Security (2010) *Risk Lexicon*, available at *www.dhs.gov/xlibrary/assets/dhs-risk-lexicon-2010.pdf.*

Annex B

Members of the Future Global Shocks Project

Steering Group

At the beginning of the project on "Future Global Shocks" a Steering Group was set up to provide overall advice to the OECD Project Team. It was composed of high-ranking experts and decision makers from public and private entities involved in the public safety, homeland security, insurance and financial sectors that contributed financially to the project. The Steering Group met four times over the course of the project (October 2009, June 2010, December 2010 and March 2011).

Chairman

Michael Oborne, Director (retired) of the OECD International Futures Programme (IFP)

The members

Canada

Jean-François Normand
Chargé de mission auprès du délégué, Délégation aux Affaires francophones et multilatérales
Délégation générale du Québec à Paris

Patricia Caris
Directrice des affaires intergouvernementales et de la coopération internationale
Ministère de la Santé et des Services sociaux
Gouvernement du Québec

Simon Décary
Ministère du Conseil exécutif
Gouvernement du Québec

Vincent LaPenna
Conseiller en affaires internationales, Direction de la planification et des politiques
Ministry of International Relations of Quebec (MRI)
Gouvernement du Québec

Marc Morin
Ministère de la Sécurité publique du Québec
Gouvernement du Québec

Céline Tremblay
Conseillère en sécurité civile
Direction générale des affaires économiques régionales
Ministère du Développement économique, de l'Innovation et de l'Exportation
Gouvernement du Québec

Line Tremblay
Chef du Service de la sécurité civile
Ministère des Transports
Gouvernement du Québec

Finland

Timo Härkönen
Director of Government Security
Preparedness Department
Prime Minister's Office

France

Préfet Yann Jounot
Directeur Planification Sécurité Nationale
Ministère de l'intérieur, de l'outre-mer et des collectivités territoriales

Alain Coursaget
Directeur adjoint de la Protection et sécurité de l'Etat
Secrétariat Général de la Défense Nationale

Guillaume Schlumberger
Directeur, Délégation à la Prospective et à la Stratégie
Ministère de l'Intérieur, de l'Outre-mer et des Collectivités territoriales

Gaël Marchand
Colonel Gendarmerie – chargé de mission
Ministère de l'intérieur, de l'outre-mer et des collectivités territoriales

Geoffrey Delcroix
Chargé de mission
Délégation à la Prospective et Sécurité de l'État
Ministère de l'Intérieur, de l'Outre-mer et des Collectivités territoriales

Emmanuel Phelut
Chargé de mission
Délégation à la Prospective et la Stratégie
Ministère de l'intérieur, de l'Outre-mer, et des Collectivités Territoriales

Republic of Korea

Cheonsik Woo
Senior Fellow
Korea Development Institute (KDI)

The Netherlands

H. W. M. (Dick) Schoof
Director General
Ministry of Security and Justice

R. W. C. (Ruth) Clabbers
Director
Ministry of Security and Justice

Henk G. Geveke
Director
Ministry of Security and Justice

Samira Lahdahda
Senior Policy Advisor
Critical Infrastructure Protection
Ministry of Security and Justice

Joris Knops
Senior Policy Advisor, National Safety and Security
Ministry of Security and Justice

Republic of Singapore

Chuan Leong Lam
Ambassador-at-Large
Ministry of Foreign Affairs

Ark Boon Lee
Director
National Security Coordination Centre, Prime Minister's Office

Ping Soon Kok
Director
National Security Coordination Centre, Prime Minister's Office

Patrick Nathan
Deputy Director
National Security Coordination Centre
Prime Minister's Office

Edna Tan
Assistant Director, Horizon Scanning Centre
National Security Coordination Centre, Prime Minister's Office

Jeremy Huang
Strategic Policy Office

Wesley Lim
Staffing Officer
National Security Coordination Centre

Sandra Ng
Staffing Officer
National Security Coordination Centre

Kim Ong-Giger
Staffing Officer
National Security Coordination Centre

United Kingdom

John Tesh
Deputy Director, Capabilities
Civil Contingencies Secretariat
Cabinet Office

Helen Tabiner
Assistant Director, Strategy, Capabilities & Performance
Civil Contingencies Secretariat
Cabinet Office

United States of America

Tina W. Gabbrielli
Director, Office of Risk Management and Analysis
National Protection and Programs Directorate
United States Department of Homeland Security

Lilly Gilmour
Section Chief, Risk Policy
Office of Risk Management and Analysis
National Protection and Programs Directorate
United States Department of Homeland Security

Private Sector

Jean-Noël Guye
Senior Vice President, Group Risk Management
Direction des Risques
AXA Group

Alice Steenland
Directeur Développement Durable Groupe
AXA Group

Ingo Zimmermann
Corporate Insurance Risk Management
EADS

Alex Wittenberg
Managing Partner, Global Head of Corporate Risk
Oliver Wyman Group

Boris Galonske
Partner
Oliver Wyman Group

Rolf Skjong
Chief Scientist, Risk & Reliability
Det Norske Veritas

Lars Erik Mangset
Researcher, DNV Research and Innovation
Det Norske Veritas

Frank Børre Pedersen
Head of Section: Business Risk
Det Norske Veritas Energy

Daniel Hofmann
Group Chief Economist
Zurich Insurance Company

Other

Aleksandar Jovanovic
CEO
European Virtual Institute for Integrated Risk Management
Germany

Contributing experts

Stefan Thurner
Section for Science of Complex Systems
Medical University of Vienna
Austria

John Casti
IIASA, Laxenburg
and The Kenos Circle, Vienna
Austria

Ortwin Renn
Professor of Environmental Sociology and Technology Assessment
University of Stuttgart
Germany

Regina Schröter
Expert
European Virtual Institute for Integrated Risk Management
Germany

Peter Sommer
Visiting Professor
Department of Management (Information Systems and Innovation Group)
London School of Economics and Political Science
United Kingdom

Ian Brown
Senior Research Fellow
Oxford Internet Institute
University of Oxford
United Kingdom

Harvey Rubin
Institute for Strategic Threat Analysis and Response
University of Pennsylvania
United States

Invited experts

Hélène Lavoix
Consultant & Researcher
France

Michel Riguidel
Professeur émérite
Télécom ParisTech
France

Erik Pruyt
Delft University of Technology
Faculty of Technology, Policy and Management
Policy Analysis Section
The Netherlands

Chien-Hsin Cheng
Science & Technology Advisor
Department of Industrial Technology
Ministry of Economic Affairs
Chinese Taipei

Ren Chain Wang
Director
Industrial Economics and Knowledge Center
Industrial Technology Research Institute
Chinese Taipei

Ching-Cheng Chang
Research Fellow
Institute of Economics, Academia Sinica
Chinese Taipei

Nancy Leveson
Professor (Engineering Systems, Aeronautics and Astronautics)
Massachusetts Institute of Technology (MIT)
United States

Tomoo Inoue
Director
Japan Water Forum, Secretariat of the Asia-Pacific Water Forum & the Northern
Water Network
Japan

OECD experts

Rolf Alter
Director
Public Governance and Territorial Development Directorate

Laurent Bernat
Administrator (Information Security and Privacy)
Information, Communications and Consumer Policy Division
Directorate for Science, Technology and Industry

Stéphane Jacobzone
Counsellor
Public Governance and Territorial Development Directorate

Edward Lazo
Principal Administrator (Radiation Protection)
OECD Nuclear Energy Agency

Patrick Love
Writer/Editor
Public Affairs and Communications Directorate

Pier Carlo Padoan
OECD Chief Economist/Deputy Secretary-General

Tracey Strange
Editorial Consultant
Public Affairs and Communications Directorate

ORGANISATION FOR ECONOMIC CO-OPERATION AND DEVELOPMENT

The OECD is a unique forum where governments work together to address the economic, social and environmental challenges of globalisation. The OECD is also at the forefront of efforts to understand and to help governments respond to new developments and concerns, such as corporate governance, the information economy and the challenges of an ageing population. The Organisation provides a setting where governments can compare policy experiences, seek answers to common problems, identify good practice and work to co-ordinate domestic and international policies.

The OECD member countries are: Australia, Austria, Belgium, Canada, Chile, the Czech Republic, Denmark, Estonia, Finland, France, Germany, Greece, Hungary, Iceland, Ireland, Israel, Italy, Japan, Korea, Luxembourg, Mexico, the Netherlands, New Zealand, Norway, Poland, Portugal, the Slovak Republic, Slovenia, Spain, Sweden, Switzerland, Turkey, the United Kingdom and the United States. The European Union takes part in the work of the OECD.

OECD Publishing disseminates widely the results of the Organisation's statistics gathering and research on economic, social and environmental issues, as well as the conventions, guidelines and standards agreed by its members.

OECD PUBLISHING, 2, rue André-Pascal, 75775 PARIS CEDEX 16
(42 2011 09 1 P) ISBN 978-92-64-09520-5 – No. 58203 2011-02